MW00896948

Ninja Slushi

Cookbook for Beginners

Simple Delicious Icy Treats Ninja Slushi Recipes with Irresistible Frozen
Magic | The Ultimate Guide to Slushie Tips & Tricks

Florence Cordray

Table of Contents

1 **Introduction**

2 **Fundamentals of the Ninja Slushi Professional Frozen Drink Maker**

13 **Chapter 1 Fruit Slushi Recipes**

24 **Chapter 2 Frozen Juice Slushi Recipes**

35 **Chapter 3 Soda-Based Slushi Recipes**

46 **Chapter 4 Tea-Based Slushi Recipes**

57 **Chapter 5 Spiked Slushi Recipes**

68 **Chapter 6 Sugar-Free Slushi Recipes**

79 **Chapter 7 Frappé Recipes**

90 **Chapter 8 Milkshake Recipes**

101 **Conclusion**

102 **Appendix 1 Measurement Conversion Chart**

103 **Appendix 2 Recipes Index**

Welcome to the Ninja Slushi Cookbook, your ultimate guide to creating refreshing, icy delights perfect for any season, especially summer! As the temperatures rise and the sun shines brightly, there's nothing quite like a slushi to cool you down. This cookbook is designed for both novices and experienced home chefs looking to explore the fun and delicious world of slushies.

In this collection, you'll discover a wide range of recipes that celebrate the vibrant flavors and refreshing textures of slushies. From classic combinations like strawberry-lime to inventive twists such as tropical mango-pineapple or zesty watermelon-basil, each recipe invites you to unleash your creativity in the kitchen. The versatile nature of slushies makes them suitable for any occasion—whether it's a backyard barbecue, a birthday party, or a simple afternoon treat on a hot day.

Using your Ninja Slushi, this cookbook provides easy-to-follow instructions that make the slushi-making process quick and enjoyable. You'll learn how to change the juices and syrups into icy perfection.

But the fun doesn't stop with summer; slushies can be enjoyed year-round! Picture a cozy winter gathering with friends, where you serve warm snacks alongside seasonal slushies infused with flavors like spiced apple or peppermint.

With the Ninja Slushi Cookbook for Beginners, you're not just making drinks—you're creating memorable experiences. So grab your Ninja Slushi Professional Frozen Drink Maker, gather your ingredients, and get ready to enjoy delightful slushies anytime, all year round!

Fundamentals of the Ninja Slushi Professional Frozen Drink Maker

The Ninja Slushi Professional Frozen Drink Maker is a versatile and innovative appliance designed to help you create a variety of frozen beverages with ease. Whether you're making slushies, frozen juices, frappés, milkshakes, or spiked drinks, this machine utilizes RapidChill Technology to achieve the perfect consistency for any drink in as little as 15–60 minutes. With five unique presets, you can adjust the temperature to suit your desired texture, allowing for customization of each frozen creation.

Designed for convenience, the Ninja Slushi Professional Frozen Drink Maker features an easy-fill port, allowing you to add liquids or mixed ingredients without hassle. The machine's self-rinse cycle simplifies cleaning, while dishwasher-safe components make maintenance effortless. Its compact design and efficient operation make it ideal for home kitchens, parties, or gatherings.

The temperature control settings ensure that each drink is frozen to perfection, and its easy-to-use dispensing system lets you serve your beverages smoothly. Whether you're a beginner or a frozen drink enthusiast, the Ninja Slushi Professional Frozen Drink Maker provides an intuitive and reliable way to craft refreshing, restaurant-quality drinks at home.

What is the Ninja Slushi Professional Frozen Drink Maker?

The Ninja Slushi Professional Frozen Drink Maker revolutionizes the way you create icy beverages, transforming your kitchen into a refreshing drink hub. This innovative appliance is designed for slushi lovers who crave the perfect blend of flavor, texture, and convenience. With its state-of-the-art features, making slushies, spiked slushies, milkshakes, frappés, and frozen juices has never been easier or more enjoyable.

At the heart of the Ninja Slushi Maker is its Rapidchill Technology, which quickly chills your ingredients while changing them into icy perfection. This means you can whip up delicious drinks in a fraction of the time compared to traditional methods. Whether you're hosting a summer party or enjoying a quiet evening at home, this machine ensures that your slushies are ready in minutes, offering an instant refreshment whenever you need it.

Another standout feature of the Ninja Slushi Maker is its user-friendly design. The intuitive controls make it easy for anyone, regardless of skill level, to create professional-quality drinks. The compact size fits neatly on your countertop, while the removable parts ensure hassle-free cleaning. With its durable construction, this appliance is built to withstand frequent use, making it a long-lasting addition to your kitchen arsenal.

Versatility is key with the Ninja Slushi Maker. It's not just for slushies; you can also create a wide range of frozen drinks, including margaritas and frozen coffees. Experimenting with different ingredients allows for endless flavor combinations, catering to all tastes and preferences.

In summary, the Ninja Slushi Professional Frozen Drink Maker with Rapidchill Technology is an essential tool for anyone who loves refreshing, icy beverages. With its quick performance, powerful capabilities, and ease of use, it opens up a world of possibilities for making delicious frozen drinks year-round. Whether it's a summer gathering or a cozy night in, this machine is sure to elevate your drink game and impress family and friends alike.

Benefits of Using It

The Ninja Slushi Professional Frozen Drink Maker with Rapidchill Technology is an innovative appliance designed to enhance your beverage experience at home. With its advanced features and user-friendly design, it offers numerous benefits that make it a valuable addition to any kitchen. Here are ten key benefits of this versatile machine:

1. Rapid Drink Preparation

Quick Cooling: The Rapidchill Technology significantly reduces the time needed to prepare frozen drinks. This means you can enjoy refreshing slushies, frappés, and milkshakes within minutes, making it perfect for spontaneous gatherings or hot summer days.

Convenience: No more waiting hours for your drinks to chill. This feature is especially useful when entertaining guests or when you simply crave a frozen treat.

2. Versatile Beverage Options

Multiple Drink Types: This machine allows you to create a wide variety of beverages, including slushies, spiked slushies, frappés, milkshakes, and frozen juices. The versatility ensures that there's something for everyone, regardless of their taste preferences.

Customization: You can experiment with different ingredients and flavors to craft unique drinks that suit your mood or occasion, whether it's a kids' party or a summer BBQ.

3. User-Friendly Interface

Simple Controls: The intuitive control panel is designed for ease of use, making it accessible for both adults and children. You don't need to be a culinary expert to whip up delicious drinks.

Adjustable Settings: Users can tailor the texture and consistency of their beverages, allowing for personalized results every time. This feature caters to individual preferences, whether you like your slushies finely crushed or coarser.

4. Large Capacity

Generous Servings: With its spacious vessel, the Ninja Slushi Maker can prepare multiple servings in one go.

This is especially beneficial when entertaining, as you can make enough drinks for the entire group.

Time-Saving: The ability to make large quantities at once reduces the time spent preparing drinks, allowing you to enjoy more time with your guests.

5. Easy to Clean

Dishwasher Safe Parts: Most components of the Ninja Slushi Maker are dishwasher safe, which simplifies the cleanup process. You can enjoy your drinks without the hassle of complicated cleaning.

Removable Container: The vessel is easily detachable, making it convenient to wash and store, thus encouraging frequent use without the dread of post-drink cleanup.

6. Compact Design

Space-Saving: Its sleek and compact design makes it easy to fit on countertops without taking up too much space. This is ideal for kitchens with limited storage or counter area.

Stylish Appearance: The modern aesthetic of the Ninja Slushi Maker adds a touch of style to your kitchen while providing functionality.

7. Durable Construction

High-Quality Materials: The appliance is built with sturdy, high-quality materials that ensure long-lasting performance. You can trust that it will withstand regular use without compromising its efficiency.

Reliable Performance: The durable construction guarantees that you can enjoy your favorite frozen drinks for years to come, making it a worthwhile investment.

8. Healthier Beverage Options

Control Over Ingredients: Making drinks at home allows you to choose healthier ingredients. You can use fresh fruits, low-sugar syrups, and natural juices to create beverages that are more nutritious than store-bought options.

Customizable Recipes: This flexibility enables you to cater to dietary preferences, including low-calorie or sugar-free options, making it easier to maintain a healthy lifestyle while enjoying delicious treats.

9. Fun for All Ages

Family-Friendly: The Ninja Slushi Maker is a fantastic addition to family gatherings. Kids and adults alike can enjoy creating their own frozen beverages, making it a fun activity for everyone.

Interactive Experience: Engaging the family in the drink-making process can enhance bonding and create lasting memories, whether it's crafting unique slushies or trying out new frappé recipes.

10. Great for Entertaining

Perfect for Parties: Whether you're hosting a birthday party, summer barbecue, or holiday celebration, the Ninja Slushi Maker allows you to impress your guests with a range of delicious frozen drinks.

Unique Drink Offerings: Stand out as a host by serving creative and refreshing beverages that can be tailored to the theme of your event, adding a special touch to any gathering.

Before First Use

To ensure your new appliance is ready for use, follow these detailed steps for a safe and efficient setup:

1. **Remove All Packaging Materials:** Begin by carefully unboxing the unit. Ensure that all packaging materials, such as plastic, foam inserts, and protective coverings, are completely removed from both the exterior and interior components.

2. **Wash All Parts:** Detach any removable parts and accessories, such as trays, containers, and any additional attachments. Wash them thoroughly in warm, soapy water to remove any manufacturing residues. Use a gentle sponge to clean all surfaces.

3. **Rinse and Air-Dry:** After washing, thoroughly rinse all parts with clean water to ensure no soap residue is left behind. Place the parts on a clean surface or drying rack and allow them to air-dry completely. Avoid using towels to dry as this may leave fibers behind.

4. **Wipe the Main Unit:** Using a soft, damp cloth, gently wipe down the control panel, motor base, and evaporator. Be sure to clean any areas that might collect dust or debris during packaging. Once wiped, allow these parts to dry fully before proceeding.

5. **Allow the Unit to Settle:** Place the appliance on a flat, stable surface, such as a countertop. Let it rest for at least 2 hours before operating. This is essential to allow the refrigerant to settle in the condenser, ensuring optimal performance and safe usage.

Important Information Before First Use:

1. **Warnings:** Make sure to carefully read and review all safety warnings at the start of the Owner's Guide before proceeding with the setup.

2. **BPA-Free Attachments:** Rest assured, all removable attachments are BPA-free, offering safer food handling.

3. **Cleaning Accessories:** While the accessories are

dishwasher-safe, avoid using the heated dry cycle, as this could damage the materials. Opt for air-drying to maintain their durability.

Using the Different Presets of the Ninja Slushi Professional Frozen Drink Maker

In order to use The Ninja Slushi Professional Frozen Drink Maker in a better way, let's take a look at its control panel.

1. **Power:** Press the button to turn the unit on or off.
2. **Rinse Cycle:** This cycle agitates the unit without cooling, helping to rinse and clean it.
3. **Presets:** The unit features 5 unique presets that use RapidChill Technology to find the perfect temperature for an ideal frozen drink.
4. **Temperature Control Setting:** Each preset starts at an optimal temperature for the best texture, but you can adjust it as needed. To create sippable frozen drinks, lower the temperature by pressing the bottom arrow on the control panel. For thicker, colder frozen drinks, raise the temperature by pressing the top arrow on the control panel.

Troubleshooting Tips

- Recipe not slushing? If your recipe hasn't reached the desired texture after 60 minutes, raise the temperature by one level. Wait 10-15 minutes, then check the texture. If needed, increase the temperature again until the desired texture is achieved.
- Slush not dispensing? Ensure the unit is filled to the max fill line and running. For a smoother dispense, lower the temperature by pressing the bottom arrow. Sippable frozen drinks will dispense more smoothly.

Here are five presets of the Ninja Slushi Professional Frozen Drink Maker.

Slush

- Designed to create classic frozen slushies from chilled liquids.
- Ideal for soft drinks, fruit juices, soda, lemonade, or sweetened water-based beverages.
- For best results, pre-chill your liquids and use the temperature control to adjust the consistency of your slush.
- Dispense the slush within 30 minutes to maintain optimal texture.

Spiked Slush

- Perfect for making frozen cocktails with alcohol, margarita, and rosé.
- Ensure that the alcohol content is between 2.8% and 16% for best results.

- Works well with premade cocktails, wine, or spirits mixed with juices or mixers.
- Dispense immediately after the cycle for a smooth, slushy consistency.

Frappé

- Ideal for changing chilled coffee or tea-based beverages into a smooth, icy frappé.
- Works best with pre-mixed or premade frappé mixtures.
- Dispense within 30 minutes after the cycle to avoid a foamy output.
- Adjust the temperature control for a thicker or thinner consistency.

Milkshake

- Specially designed for milk-based drinks such as milkshakes.
- Use pre-chilled milk, ice cream, or milkshake bases for a creamy and thick consistency.
- Make sure to dispense within 30 minutes to avoid excess foam or separation.
- Adjust settings for a desired thickness of your milkshake.

Frozen Juice

- Perfect for turning fruit juices into refreshing frozen beverages.
- Use chilled, sweetened juices for best results and a smooth slushy texture.
- Adjust the temperature control to suit the level of ice in your frozen juice.
- For optimal flavor, consume the drink immediately after dispensing.

Step-By-Step Instructions

1. Ensure all parts are thoroughly cleaned and the motor base is placed level on a flat, solid surface.
2. Install the condensation catch under the evaporator by sliding it into the rail grooves.
3. Install the auger by sliding it over the evaporator and rotating it until it locks into place on the pin.
4. With the bail handle up, slide the vessel over the installed auger and evaporator.
5. Secure the vessel by pushing the bail handle down to lock it in place.
6. Insert the drip tray in front of the motor base until it clicks into place. Plug the unit in.
7. Open the cover on top of the vessel.
8. Add liquid(s) or mixed ingredients through the easy fill port, then close the cover.
9. Press the power button to turn the unit on.
10. Select your desired preset.
11. The preset will begin at the default/optimal temperature for the ideal texture. Adjust the temperature if needed for your perfect frozen drink.

Notes:

- The Temperature Control Setting LEDs will pulse while freezing; once the desired temperature is reached, the LEDs will stay solid, and the unit will beep.
- Drinks may take 15–60 minutes to freeze, depending

on the ingredients, volume, and starting temperature.

- Pre-frozen ingredients taste sweeter, but freezing will balance out the sweetness.

12. Place a cup on the drip tray, under the handle.

13. To dispense, gently pull the handle. Release the handle to stop.

14. Enjoy your frozen drink!

Note: Do not turn off the preset until all the frozen drink has been dispensed.

Helpful Tips for Using the Ninja Slushi Professional Frozen Drink Maker

To ensure optimal performance and longevity of your Ninja Slushi Professional Frozen Drink Maker, follow these detailed instructions:

1. **Keep Unit Upright:** Before using your unit for the first time, ensure that it remains upright for at least 2 hours. This allows the internal components, particularly the refrigerant, to settle properly and guarantees safe operation.

2. **Avoid Adding Hot Ingredients:** Never add hot ingredients to the unit, as this can affect the cooling mechanism and damage the machine. Always ensure that all liquids or mixed ingredients are at room temperature or cooler.

3. **Do Not Add Ice or Solid Ingredients:** The unit is not designed to process ice, frozen fruit, solid fruit pieces, or ice cream. These hard ingredients can cause the blades to jam or damage internal parts. Use only liquid or soft, pre-mixed mixtures.

4. **Sweetness of Pre-Frozen Ingredients:** Pre-frozen ingredients may taste sweeter before being processed. However, there's no need to worry if your mixture seems overly sweet. After being slushed and frozen, the sweetness level typically reduces, making the drink balanced.

5. **Ensure Proper Sugar Content:** Every input must include at least 4% sugar content. This helps the freezing process function correctly and gives your drink the right consistency.

6. **Alcohol Percentage for Spiked Slush:** If using the Spiked Slush preset, ensure that premade mixtures contain between 2.8% and 16% alcohol. This range allows for proper freezing and ensures the drink maintains the correct texture.

7. **Pre-Chill Ingredients:** For best results, pre-chill any liquid or mixed ingredients before adding them to the unit. This helps the machine reach the desired frozen texture more quickly.

8. **Chill Serving Glasses:** For an extra frosty experience, chill your serving glasses in the fridge or freezer before dispensing your drink. This will maintain the temperature and consistency of the frozen beverage.

9. **Use Temperature Control:** The unit offers temperature control settings. Adjust these settings to achieve your ideal frozen drink texture, whether you prefer a lighter slush or a thicker, more frozen consistency.

10. **Dispense Milkshakes and Frappés Promptly:** When using the Milkshake or Frappé preset, make sure to dispense the contents within 30 minutes of the programme ending to avoid a foamy texture in your drink.

11. **Fill to Max Line for Best Results:** For the best dispensing experience, always fill the unit to its max-fill line of 64 oz. This ensures that the machine operates at optimal capacity for smoother, more consistent results.

12. **Run Time:** The unit can be run for up to 12 hours continuously, providing ample time to serve multiple batches of frozen drinks at parties or gatherings.

13. **Cleaning and Dishwasher Use:** All parts of the unit, except the motor base and evaporator, are dishwasher safe. However, avoid using the heated dry cycle in the dishwasher as this could damage the materials. Hand drying is recommended.

14. **Input Capacity Requirements:** The minimum amount of liquid input for the unit is 16 oz (2 cups), and the maximum capacity is 64 oz (8 cups). Avoid exceeding or underfilling these limits to maintain optimal performance.

By following these helpful tips, you'll ensure that your Ninja Slushi Professional Frozen Drink Maker operates smoothly and produces delicious, high-quality frozen beverages.

Cleaning and Caring for the Ninja Slushi Professional Frozen Drink Maker

Proper cleaning and care of the Ninja Slushi Professional Frozen Drink Maker are crucial for maintaining its performance, hygiene, and longevity. Regular cleaning ensures that your frozen drinks are free from residue or leftover flavors, preventing any unwanted contamination. By washing the components thoroughly after each use, you avoid the build-up of ingredients that could lead to clogging or mechanical issues, ensuring the machine operates smoothly.

Using the Rinse Cycle
Note: Liquids from the rinse cycle will dispense quickly. Use a large cup or bowl to catch the liquid.
This cycle agitates without cooling to rinse the unit. After the rinse cycle, hand-wash or use a dishwasher to clean all parts.
Steps:

1. Dispense any remaining frozen drink.
2. Stop the current preset and press the RINSE button.
3. Fill the vessel with hot water up to the max fill line (64 oz).
4. Slowly dispense the water immediately after filling.
5. Press the RINSE button again to stop the cycle.
6. Turn the unit off by pressing the power button.

Note: Repeat the rinse cycle if necessary to remove any remaining frozen drink from the evaporator.

Disassembly and Cleaning

For best results, use the rinse cycle before disassembling and cleaning.

Steps:

1. Unlock the bail handle, pull it forward, and gently remove the vessel. Tip it downward to avoid spilling remaining liquid.
2. Slide the auger off the evaporator and set it aside.
3. Wipe the evaporator with a sanitized or warm, damp cloth.
4. Remove the condensation catch and set it aside, as it may contain residual liquid.
5. Wipe down the area underneath the evaporator with a sanitized or warm, damp cloth.
6. Remove the drip tray and/or spout shroud if necessary.
7. **Note:** The drip tray cover can be removed for easier cleaning.
8. Hand-wash all parts in hot, soapy water, or place them in the dishwasher.
9. Wipe the motor base with a sanitized or warm, damp cloth.
10. Allow all parts to dry completely before reassembling or storing the unit.

Storing the Unit

1. For cord storage, use the hook-and-loop fastener located near the back of the motor base.
2. DO NOT wrap the cord around the bottom of the base.
3. Store the unit upright with all parts assembled.

4. Hang the drip tray on the left side of the unit for storage.

5. When moving the unit, lift from the bottom of the motor base.

6. DO NOT store ingredients inside the vessel.

By paying attention to both the cleanliness and condition of your machine, you ensure it continues to produce fresh, delicious frozen beverages while remaining safe to use. Proper care not only maximizes the performance of the machine but also safeguards your health by preventing bacteria or mold from forming in areas that may be hard to clean if neglected.

Frequently Asked Questions

1. What is the Ninja Slushi Professional Frozen Drink Maker?

The Ninja Slushi Maker is a specialized appliance designed for creating slushies, frozen drinks, slushies, frappés, milkshakes, and more. It features Rapidchill Technology, which quickly chills ingredients to create refreshing beverages in a fraction of the time compared to traditional methods.

2. How does Rapidchill Technology work?

Rapidchill Technology utilizes a powerful freezing chamber that cools ingredients rapidly. This process ensures your drinks maintain their flavor and texture while achieving the desired slushy consistency quickly, making it perfect for spontaneous gatherings or summer days.

3. What types of drinks can I make with the Ninja Slushi Maker?

You can create a variety of beverages, including classic fruit slushies, frappés, frozen cocktails, milkshakes, and even non-alcoholic drinks for kids. The versatility allows for endless flavor combinations, making it easy to cater to different tastes.

4. How do I operate the Ninja Slushi Maker?

Operating the Ninja Slushi Maker is straightforward. Simply add your ingredients to the vessel, select the desired setting on the control panel, and let the machine do the work. The intuitive interface makes it easy for anyone to create delicious frozen drinks.

5. What is the capacity of the vessel?

The vessel has a generous capacity, allowing you to create multiple servings in one go. This makes it ideal for parties, family gatherings, or simply preparing a refreshing drink for yourself.

6. Is the Ninja Slushi Maker easy to clean?

Yes! The Ninja Slushi Maker is designed for easy cleaning. Most parts are detachable and dishwasher safe, making cleanup a breeze after your slushi-making session. This convenience ensures you can spend more time enjoying your drinks and less time on maintenance.

7. What kind of ingredients should I avoid using?

While the Ninja Slushi Maker is versatile, it's best to avoid hard, solid items like ice cubes that are larger than the recommended size, as they may damage the blades or motor. Stick to softer ingredients and liquids to ensure the best results.

8. Can I use carbonated beverages in the Ninja Slushi Maker?

Yes, you can use carbonated beverages to create fizzy slushies. However, it's recommended to add the carbonated drink after the slushi has been combined to prevent excessive fizzing during the mixing process. This way, you'll enjoy a refreshing slushy without the risk of overflow.

9. What safety features does the Ninja Slushi Maker have?

The Ninja Slushi Maker is equipped with several safety features, including a secure lid that prevents spills and a motor protection system that stops the machine if it overheats or is overloaded. These features ensure safe operation while you create your favorite frozen drinks.

10. Is there a specific way to store the Ninja Slushi Maker when not in use?

To keep your Ninja Slushi Maker in optimal condition, store it in a cool, dry place away from direct sunlight. Ensure it's clean and dry before storing. If you have limited counter space, it's compact enough to fit in most cabinets, making it easy to store when not in use.

Chapter 1 Fruit Slushi Recipes

Refreshing Lemonade Slushi…………………………… 14

Blue Raspberry Fruit Punch Slushi ………………… 14

Cranberry Strawberry Slushi ……………………… 15

Mango Pineapple Tropical Slushi …………………… 15

Mango Lemonade Slushi ……………………… 16

Cranberry and Apple Slushi …………………… 16

Sweet Peach Slushi…………………………………… 17

White Cranberry Slushi ……………………………… 17

Homemade Pomegranate Limeade Slushi ………… 18

Pineapple Coconut Slushi …………………………… 18

Fruit Punch Slushi…………………………………… 19

Lemon Seltzer Slushi ………………………………… 19

Sweet-Sour Blue Lemonade Slushi ………………… 20

Orange Lemonade Slushi …………………………… 20

Cranberry Limeade Slushi ………………………… 21

Citrus Peach Slushi ………………………………… 21

Mango Coconut Lemonade Slushi ………………… 22

Simple Strawberry Slushi …………………………… 22

Homemade Pineapple Coconut Slushi ……………… 23

Lemony Cherry Seltzer Slushi ……………………… 23

Refreshing Lemonade Slushi

Servings: 8

Ingredients:

7½ cups sweetened lemonade

⅓ cup white sugar

Preparation:

1. Put the lemonade and sugar into a large-sized pitcher and whisk to dissolve the sugar.
2. Pour the mixture into the vessel of Ninja Slushi.
3. Select "SLUSH". The preset will start at the default/optimal temperature for ideal texture.
4. If desired, adjust the temperature.
5. Once the frozen drink reaches the optimal temperature, the unit will beep.
6. Enjoy immediately.

Blue Raspberry Fruit Punch Slushi

Servings: 8

Ingredients:

7½ cups blue raspberry fruit punch

⅓ cup white sugar

Preparation:

1. Put the fruit punch and sugar into a large-sized pitcher and whisk to dissolve the sugar.
2. Pour the mixture into the vessel of Ninja Slushi.
3. Select "SLUSH". The preset will start at the default/optimal temperature for ideal texture.
4. If desired, adjust the temperature.
5. Once the frozen drink reaches the optimal temperature, the unit will beep.
6. Enjoy immediately.

Cranberry Strawberry Slushi

Servings: 8

Ingredients:

5 cups sweetened lemonade

2¾ cups cranberry-strawberry juice

⅓ cup white sugar

Preparation:

1. Put all ingredients into a large-sized pitcher and whisk to dissolve the sugar.
2. Pour the mixture into the vessel of Ninja Slushi.
3. Select "SLUSH". The preset will start at the default/optimal temperature for ideal texture.
4. If desired, adjust the temperature.
5. Once the frozen drink reaches the optimal temperature, the unit will beep.
6. Enjoy immediately.

Mango Pineapple Tropical Slushi

Servings: 8

Ingredients:

3 cups mango margarita mix

3 cups water

¾ cup lime juice

¾ cup pineapple juice

⅓ cup white sugar

Preparation:

1. Put all ingredients into a large-sized pitcher and whisk to dissolve the sugar.
2. Pour the mixture into the vessel of Ninja Slushi.
3. Select "SLUSH". The preset will start at the default/optimal temperature for ideal texture.
4. If desired, adjust the temperature.
5. Once the frozen drink reaches the optimal temperature, the unit will beep.
6. Enjoy immediately.

Mango Lemonade Slushi

Servings: 8

Ingredients:

5 cups sweetened lemonade

2¾ cups mango nectar

¼ cup white sugar

Preparation:

1. Put all ingredients into a large-sized pitcher and whisk to dissolve the sugar.
2. Pour the mixture into the vessel of Ninja Slushi.
3. Select "SLUSH". The preset will start at the default/optimal temperature for ideal texture.
4. If desired, adjust the temperature.
5. Once the frozen drink reaches the optimal temperature, the unit will beep.
6. Enjoy immediately.

Cranberry and Apple Slushi

Servings: 8

Ingredients:

8 cups cranberry apple drink

⅓ cup white sugar

Preparation:

1. Put the cranberry apple drink and sugar into a large-sized pitcher and whisk to dissolve the sugar.
2. Pour the mixture into the vessel of Ninja Slushi.
3. Select "SLUSH". The preset will start at the default/optimal temperature for ideal texture.
4. If desired, adjust the temperature.
5. Once the frozen drink reaches the optimal temperature, the unit will beep.
6. Enjoy immediately.

Sweet Peach Slushi

Ingredients:

8 cups peach drink   ⅓ cup white sugar

Preparation:

1. Put the peach drink and sugar into a large-sized pitcher and whisk to dissolve the sugar.
2. Pour the mixture into the vessel of Ninja Slushi.
3. Select "SLUSH". The preset will start at the default/optimal temperature for ideal texture.
4. If desired, adjust the temperature.
5. Once the frozen drink reaches the optimal temperature, the unit will beep.
6. Enjoy immediately.

White Cranberry Slushi

Servings: 8

Ingredients:

8 cups white cranberry drink   ⅓ cup white sugar

Preparation:

1. Put the cranberry drink and sugar into a large-sized pitcher and whisk to dissolve the sugar.
2. Pour the mixture into the vessel of Ninja Slushi.
3. Select "SLUSH". The preset will start at the default/optimal temperature for ideal texture.
4. If desired, adjust the temperature.
5. Once the frozen drink reaches the optimal temperature, the unit will beep.
6. Enjoy immediately.

Homemade Pomegranate Limeade Slushi

Servings: 8

Ingredients:

5 cups sweetened limeade
2¾ cups pomegranate juice

⅓ cup white sugar

Preparation:

1. Put all ingredients into a large-sized pitcher and whisk to dissolve the sugar.
2. Pour the mixture into the vessel of Ninja Slushi.
3. Select "SLUSH". The preset will start at the default/optimal temperature for ideal texture.
4. If desired, adjust the temperature.
5. Once the frozen drink reaches the optimal temperature, the unit will beep.
6. Enjoy immediately.

Pineapple Coconut Slushi

Servings: 8

Ingredients:

3⅓ cups canned unsweetened coconut milk
3⅓ cups sweetened limeade

1 cup pineapple juice
⅓ cup white sugar

Preparation:

1. Put all ingredients into a large-sized pitcher and whisk to dissolve the sugar.
2. Pour the mixture into the vessel of Ninja Slushi.
3. Select "SLUSH". The preset will start at the default/optimal temperature for ideal texture.
4. If desired, adjust the temperature.
5. Once the frozen drink reaches the optimal temperature, the unit will beep.
6. Enjoy immediately.

Fruit Punch Slushi

Servings: 8

Ingredients:

7½ cups fruit punch

⅓ cup white sugar

Preparation:

1. Put the fruit punch and sugar into a large-sized pitcher and whisk to dissolve the sugar.
2. Pour the mixture into the vessel of Ninja Slushi.
3. Select "SLUSH". The preset will start at the default/optimal temperature for ideal texture.
4. If desired, adjust the temperature.
5. Once the frozen drink reaches the optimal temperature, the unit will beep.
6. Enjoy immediately.

Lemon Seltzer Slushi

Servings: 8

Ingredients:

8 cups lemon seltzer water

⅓ cup white sugar

Preparation:

1. Put the lemon seltzer water and sugar into a large-sized pitcher and whisk to dissolve the sugar.
2. Pour the mixture into the vessel of Ninja Slushi.
3. Select "SLUSH". The preset will start at the default/optimal temperature for ideal texture.
4. If desired, adjust the temperature.
5. Once the frozen drink reaches the optimal temperature, the unit will beep.
6. Enjoy immediately.

Sweet-Sour Blue Lemonade Slushi

Servings: 8

Ingredients:

5 cups blue lemonade

⅔ cup lemon juice

1⅔ cups sweet and sour mix

⅓ cup white sugar

Preparation:

1. Put all ingredients into a large-sized pitcher and whisk to dissolve the sugar.
2. Pour the mixture into the vessel of Ninja Slushi.
3. Select "SLUSH". The preset will start at the default/optimal temperature for ideal texture.
4. If desired, adjust the temperature.
5. Once the frozen drink reaches the optimal temperature, the unit will beep.
6. Enjoy immediately.

Orange Lemonade Slushi

Servings: 8

Ingredients:

5 cups sweetened lemonade

2¾ cups orange juice

⅓ cup white sugar

Preparation:

1. Put all ingredients into a large-sized pitcher and whisk to dissolve the sugar.
2. Pour the mixture into the vessel of Ninja Slushi.
3. Select "SLUSH". The preset will start at the default/optimal temperature for ideal texture.
4. If desired, adjust the temperature.
5. Once the frozen drink reaches the optimal temperature, the unit will beep.
6. Enjoy immediately.

Cranberry Limeade Slushi

Ingredients:

5¾ cups cranberry juice
1½ cups limeade

⅓ cup white sugar

Preparation:

1. Put all ingredients into a large-sized pitcher and whisk to dissolve the sugar.
2. Pour the mixture into the vessel of Ninja Slushi.
3. Select "SLUSH". The preset will start at the default/optimal temperature for ideal texture.
4. If desired, adjust the temperature.
5. Once the frozen drink reaches the optimal temperature, the unit will beep.
6. Enjoy immediately.

Citrus Peach Slushi

Ingredients:

3 cups peach margarita mix
3 cups water
¾ cup lemon juice

¾ cup orange juice
⅓ cup white sugar

Preparation:

1. Put all ingredients into a large-sized pitcher and whisk to dissolve the sugar.
2. Pour the mixture into the vessel of Ninja Slushi.
3. Select "SLUSH". The preset will start at the default/optimal temperature for ideal texture.
4. If desired, adjust the temperature.
5. Once the frozen drink reaches the optimal temperature, the unit will beep.
6. Enjoy immediately.

Mango Coconut Lemonade Slushi

Servings: 8

Ingredients:

3⅓ cups canned unsweetened coconut milk

3⅓ cups sweetened lemonade

1 cup mango juice

⅓ cup white sugar

Preparation:

1. Put all ingredients into a large-sized pitcher and whisk to dissolve the sugar.
2. Pour the mixture into the vessel of Ninja Slushi.
3. Select "SLUSH". The preset will start at the default/optimal temperature for ideal texture.
4. If desired, adjust the temperature.
5. Once the frozen drink reaches the optimal temperature, the unit will beep.
6. Enjoy immediately.

Simple Strawberry Slushi

Servings: 8

Ingredients:

8 cups strawberry drink

⅓ cup white sugar

Preparation:

1. Put the strawberry drink and sugar into a large-sized pitcher and whisk to dissolve the sugar.
2. Pour the mixture into the vessel of Ninja Slushi.
3. Select "SLUSH". The preset will start at the default/optimal temperature for ideal texture.
4. If desired, adjust the temperature.
5. Once the frozen drink reaches the optimal temperature, the unit will beep.
6. Enjoy immediately.

Homemade Pineapple Coconut Slushi

Servings: 8

Ingredients:

7½ cups pineapple coconut sports drink

⅓ cup white sugar

Preparation:

1. Put the sports drink and sugar into a large-sized pitcher and whisk to dissolve the sugar.
2. Pour the mixture into the vessel of Ninja Slushi.
3. Select "SLUSH". The preset will start at the default/optimal temperature for ideal texture.
4. If desired, adjust the temperature.
5. Once the frozen drink reaches the optimal temperature, the unit will beep.
6. Enjoy immediately.

Lemony Cherry Seltzer Slushi

Servings: 8

Ingredients:

5 (12-ounce) cans cherry seltzer water
⅓ cup lemon juice

⅓ cup white sugar

Preparation:

1. Put all ingredients into a large-sized pitcher and whisk to dissolve the sugar.
2. Pour the mixture into the vessel of Ninja Slushi.
3. Select "SLUSH". The preset will start at the default/optimal temperature for ideal texture.
4. If desired, adjust the temperature.
5. Once the frozen drink reaches the optimal temperature, the unit will beep.
6. Enjoy immediately.

Chapter 2 Frozen Juice Slushi Recipes

Watermelon Frozen Juice Slushi 25

Grapefruit Frozen Juice Slushi.......................... 25

Cranberry Mango Frozen Juice Slushi 26

Apple Cider Frozen Juice Slushi 26

Sweet Mango Frozen Juice Slushi...................... 27

Cranberry Watermelon Frozen Juice Slushi 27

Cranberry-Orange Frozen Juice Slushi 28

Easy Cherry Frozen Juice Slushi 28

Pineapple Frozen Juice Slushi 29

Cranberry Concord Grape Frozen Juice Slushi 29

Orange Pineapple Frozen Juice Slushi 30

Berry Frozen Juice Slushi 30

Mango Frozen Juice Slushi 31

Orange Frozen Juice Slushi 31

Tropical Pineapple Mango Frozen Juice Slushi 32

Cranberry Frozen Juice Slushi.......................... 32

Pomegranate Orange Frozen Juice Slushi 33

Cranberry Pineapple Frozen Juice Slushi 33

Raspberry Frozen Juice Slushi 34

Easy Pineapple Orange Frozen Juice Slushi 34

Watermelon Frozen Juice Slushi

Servings: 8

Ingredients:

8 cups watermelon juice   ⅓ cup white sugar

Preparation:

1. Put the watermelon juice and sugar into a large-sized pitcher and whisk to dissolve the sugar.
2. Pour the mixture into the vessel of Ninja Slushi.
3. Select "FROZEN JUICE". The preset will start at the default temperature for ideal texture.
4. If desired, adjust the temperature.
5. Once the frozen drink reaches the optimal temperature, the unit will beep.
6. Enjoy immediately.

Grapefruit Frozen Juice Slushi

Servings: 8

Ingredients:

8 cups grapefruit juice   ⅓ cup white sugar

Preparation:

1. Put the grapefruit juice and sugar into a large-sized pitcher and whisk to dissolve the sugar.
2. Pour the mixture into the vessel of Ninja Slushi.
3. Select "FROZEN JUICE". The preset will start at the default temperature for ideal texture.
4. If desired, adjust the temperature.
5. Once the frozen drink reaches the optimal temperature, the unit will beep.
6. Enjoy immediately.

Cranberry Mango Frozen Juice Slushi

Servings: 8

Ingredients:

8 cups cranberry mango Juice   ⅓ cup white sugar

Preparation:

1. Put the cranberry mango juice and sugar into a large-sized pitcher and whisk to dissolve the sugar.
2. Pour the mixture into the vessel of Ninja Slushi.
3. Select "FROZEN JUICE". The preset will start at the default temperature for ideal texture.
4. If desired, adjust the temperature.
5. Once the frozen drink reaches the optimal temperature, the unit will beep.
6. Enjoy immediately.

Apple Cider Frozen Juice Slushi

Servings: 8

Ingredients:

7½ cups apple cider   ⅓ cup white sugar

Preparation:

1. Put the apple cider and sugar into a large-sized pitcher and whisk to dissolve the sugar.
2. Pour the mixture into the vessel of Ninja Slushi.
3. Select "FROZEN JUICE". The preset will start at the default temperature for ideal texture.
4. If desired, adjust the temperature.
5. Once the frozen drink reaches the optimal temperature, the unit will beep.
6. Enjoy immediately.

Sweet Mango Frozen Juice Slushi

Servings: 8

Ingredients:

7½ cups mango juice   ¼ cup white sugar

Preparation:

1. Put the mango juice and sugar into a large-sized pitcher and whisk to dissolve the sugar.
2. Pour the mixture into the vessel of Ninja Slushi.
3. Select "FROZEN JUICE". The preset will start at the default temperature for ideal texture.
4. If desired, adjust the temperature.
5. Once the frozen drink reaches the optimal temperature, the unit will beep.
6. Enjoy immediately.

Cranberry Watermelon Frozen Juice Slushi

Servings: 8

Ingredients:

8 cups cranberry watermelon juice   ⅓ cup white sugar

Preparation:

1. Put the cranberry watermelon juice and sugar into a large-sized pitcher and whisk to dissolve the sugar.
2. Pour the mixture into the vessel of Ninja Slushi.
3. Select "FROZEN JUICE". The preset will start at the default temperature for ideal texture.
4. If desired, adjust the temperature.
5. Once the frozen drink reaches the optimal temperature, the unit will beep.
6. Enjoy immediately.

Cranberry-Orange Frozen Juice Slushi

Servings: 8

Ingredients:

5 cups orange juice

2¾ cups cranberry juice

⅓ cup white sugar

Preparation:

1. Put all ingredients into a large-sized pitcher and whisk to dissolve the sugar.
2. Pour the mixture into the vessel of Ninja Slushi.
3. Select "FROZEN JUICE". The preset will start at the default temperature for ideal texture.
4. If desired, adjust the temperature.
5. Once the frozen drink reaches the optimal temperature, the unit will beep.
6. Enjoy immediately.

Easy Cherry Frozen Juice Slushi

Servings: 8

Ingredients:

7½ cups cherry juice

⅓ cup white sugar

Preparation:

1. Put the cherry juice and sugar into a large-sized pitcher and whisk to dissolve the sugar.
2. Pour the mixture into the vessel of Ninja Slushi.
3. Select "FROZEN JUICE". The preset will start at the default temperature for ideal texture.
4. If desired, adjust the temperature.
5. Once the frozen drink reaches the optimal temperature, the unit will beep.
6. Enjoy immediately.

Pineapple Frozen Juice Slushi

Servings: 8

Ingredients:

7½ cups pineapple juice   ⅓ cup white sugar

Preparation:

1. Put the pineapple juice and sugar into a large-sized pitcher and whisk to dissolve the sugar.
2. Pour the mixture into the vessel of Ninja Slushi.
3. Select "FROZEN JUICE". The preset will start at the default temperature for ideal texture.
4. If desired, adjust the temperature.
5. Once the frozen drink reaches the optimal temperature, the unit will beep.
6. Enjoy immediately.

Cranberry Concord Grape Frozen Juice Slushi

Servings: 8

Ingredients:

8 cups cranberry concord grape juice

Preparation:

1. Put the juice into the vessel of Ninja Slushi.
2. Select "FROZEN JUICE". Preset will start at the default temperature for ideal texture.
3. If desired, adjust the temperature.
4. Once the frozen drink reaches the optimal temperature, the unit will beep.
5. Enjoy immediately.

Orange Pineapple Frozen Juice Slushi

Servings: 8

Ingredients:

4 cups orange juice
4 cups pineapple juice

⅓ cup white sugar

Preparation:

1. Put all ingredients into a large-sized pitcher and whisk to dissolve the sugar.
2. Pour the mixture into the vessel of Ninja Slushi.
3. Select "FROZEN JUICE". The preset will start at the default temperature for ideal texture.
4. If desired, adjust the temperature.
5. Once the frozen drink reaches the optimal temperature, the unit will beep.
6. Enjoy immediately.

Berry Frozen Juice Slushi

Servings: 8

Ingredients:

7½ cups bottled berry smoothie

⅓ cup white sugar

Preparation:

1. Put the berry smoothie and sugar into a large-sized pitcher and whisk to dissolve the sugar.
2. Pour the mixture into the vessel of Ninja Slushi.
3. Select "FROZEN JUICE". The preset will start at the default temperature for ideal texture.
4. If desired, adjust the temperature.
5. Once the frozen drink reaches the optimal temperature, the unit will beep.
6. Enjoy immediately.

Mango Frozen Juice Slushi

Servings: 8

Ingredients:

7½ cups bottled mango smoothie   ⅓ cup white sugar

Preparation:

1. Put the mango smoothie and sugar into a large-sized pitcher and whisk to dissolve the sugar.
2. Pour the mixture into the vessel of Ninja Slushi.
3. Select "FROZEN JUICE". The preset will start at the default temperature for ideal texture.
4. If desired, adjust the temperature.
5. Once the frozen drink reaches the optimal temperature, the unit will beep.
6. Enjoy immediately.

Orange Frozen Juice Slushi

Servings: 8

Ingredients:

8 cups orange juice   ⅓ cup white sugar

Preparation:

1. Put the orange juice and sugar into a large-sized pitcher and whisk to dissolve the sugar.
2. Pour the mixture into the vessel of Ninja Slushi.
3. Select "FROZEN JUICE". The preset will start at the default temperature for ideal texture.
4. If desired, adjust the temperature.
5. Once the frozen drink reaches the optimal temperature, the unit will beep.
6. Enjoy immediately.

Tropical Pineapple Mango Frozen Juice Slushi

Servings: 8

Ingredients:

8 cups pineapple mango juice drink   ¼ cup white sugar

Preparation:

1. Put the juice drink and sugar into a large-sized pitcher and whisk to dissolve the sugar.
2. Pour the mixture into the vessel of Ninja Slushi.
3. Select "FROZEN JUICE". The preset will start at the default temperature for ideal texture.
4. If desired, adjust the temperature.
5. Once the frozen drink reaches the optimal temperature, the unit will beep.
6. Enjoy immediately.

Cranberry Frozen Juice Slushi

Servings: 8

Ingredients:

8 cups cranberry juice   ⅓ cup white sugar

Preparation:

1. Put the cranberry juice and sugar into a large-sized pitcher and whisk to dissolve the sugar.
2. Pour the mixture into the vessel of Ninja Slushi.
3. Select "FROZEN JUICE". The preset will start at the default temperature for ideal texture.
4. If desired, adjust the temperature.
5. Once the frozen drink reaches the optimal temperature, the unit will beep.
6. Enjoy immediately.

Pomegranate Orange Frozen Juice Slushi

Servings: 8

Ingredients:

5 cups orange juice
2¾ cups pomegranate juice

⅓ cup white sugar

Preparation:

1. Put all ingredients into a large-sized pitcher and whisk to dissolve the sugar.
2. Pour the mixture into the vessel of Ninja Slushi.
3. Select "FROZEN JUICE". The preset will start at the default temperature for ideal texture.
4. If desired, adjust the temperature.
5. Once the frozen drink reaches the optimal temperature, the unit will beep.
6. Enjoy immediately.

Cranberry Pineapple Frozen Juice Slushi

Servings: 8

Ingredients:

8 cups cranberry pineapple juice

⅓ cup white sugar

Preparation:

1. Put the cranberry pineapple juice and sugar into a large-sized pitcher and whisk to dissolve the sugar.
2. Pour the mixture into the vessel of Ninja Slushi.
3. Select "FROZEN JUICE". The preset will start at the default temperature for ideal texture.
4. If desired, adjust the temperature.
5. Once the frozen drink reaches the optimal temperature, the unit will beep.
6. Enjoy immediately.

Raspberry Frozen Juice Slushi

Servings: 8

Ingredients:

8 cups raspberry juice   ⅓ cup white sugar

Preparation:

1. Put the raspberry juice and sugar into a large-sized pitcher and whisk to dissolve the sugar.
2. Pour the mixture into the vessel of Ninja Slushi.
3. Select "FROZEN JUICE". The preset will start at the default temperature for ideal texture.
4. If desired, adjust the temperature.
5. Once the frozen drink reaches the optimal temperature, the unit will beep.
6. Enjoy immediately.

Easy Pineapple Orange Frozen Juice Slushi

Servings: 8

Ingredients:

5 cups orange juice   ⅓ cup white sugar
2¾ cups pineapple juice

Preparation:

1. Put all ingredients into a large-sized pitcher and whisk to dissolve the sugar.
2. Pour the mixture into the vessel of Ninja Slushi.
3. Select "FROZEN JUICE". The preset will start at the default temperature for ideal texture.
4. If desired, adjust the temperature.
5. Once the frozen drink reaches the optimal temperature, the unit will beep.
6. Enjoy immediately.

Chapter 3 Soda-Based Slushi Recipes

Vanilla Cotton Candy Soda Slushi 36

Lemon Lime Soda Slushi 36

Simple Cream Soda Slushi 37

Ginger Ale Soda Slushi 37

Citrus Fruit Punch Soda Slushi 38

Orange Soda Slushi 38

Root Beer Soda Slushi 39

Grape Soda Slushi 39

Lemon Cola Soda Slushi 40

Lemon Probiotic Soda Slushi 40

Lime Cherry Cola Soda Slushi 41

Apricot Soda Slushi 41

Sweet Pomegranate Soda Slushi 42

Lime Cola Soda Slushi 42

Grapefruit Soda Slushi 43

Blackberry Soda Slushi 43

Chocolate Soda Slushi 44

Apple Beer Slushi 44

Red Cream Soda Slushi 45

Cranberry Soda Slushi 45

Vanilla Cotton Candy Soda Slushi

Servings: 8

Ingredients:

2½ cups lemon lime soda

4⅓ cups water

3 (3-ounce) bags cotton candy

⅔ teaspoon vanilla extract

Preparation:

1. Put all ingredients into a large-sized pitcher and whisk to dissolve the cotton candy.
2. Pour the mixture into the vessel of Ninja Slushi.
3. Select "SLUSH". The preset will start at the default/optimal temperature for ideal texture.
4. If desired, adjust the temperature.
5. Once the frozen drink reaches the optimal temperature, the unit will beep.
6. Enjoy immediately.

Lemon Lime Soda Slushi

Servings: 8

Ingredients:

5 (12-oz) cans lemon-lime soda

⅓ cup white sugar

Preparation:

1. Put the lemon-lime soda and sugar into a large-sized pitcher and whisk to dissolve the sugar.
2. Pour the mixture into the vessel of Ninja Slushi.
3. Select "SLUSH". The preset will start at the default/optimal temperature for ideal texture.
4. If desired, adjust the temperature.
5. Once the frozen drink reaches the optimal temperature, the unit will beep.
6. Enjoy immediately.

Simple Cream Soda Slushi

Servings: 8

Ingredients:

5 (12-ounce) cans cream soda   ⅓ cup white sugar

Preparation:

1. Put the cream soda and sugar into a large-sized pitcher and whisk to dissolve the sugar.
2. Pour the mixture into the vessel of Ninja Slushi.
3. Select "SLUSH". The preset will start at the default/optimal temperature for ideal texture.
4. If desired, adjust the temperature.
5. Once the frozen drink reaches the optimal temperature, the unit will beep.
6. Enjoy immediately.

Ginger Ale Soda Slushi

Servings: 8

Ingredients:

5 (12-ounce) cans ginger ale soda   ⅓ cup white sugar

Preparation:

1. Put the ginger ale soda and sugar into a large-sized pitcher and whisk to dissolve the sugar.
2. Pour the mixture into the vessel of Ninja Slushi.
3. Select "SLUSH". The preset will start at the default/optimal temperature for ideal texture.
4. If desired, adjust the temperature.
5. Once the frozen drink reaches the optimal temperature, the unit will beep.
6. Enjoy immediately.

Citrus Fruit Punch Soda Slushi

Servings: 8

Ingredients:

5 cups lemon-lime soda
2¾ cups fruit punch

⅓ cup white sugar

Preparation:

1. Put all ingredients into a large-sized pitcher and whisk to dissolve the sugar.
2. Pour the mixture into the vessel of Ninja Slushi.
3. Select "SLUSH". The preset will start at the default/optimal temperature for ideal texture.
4. If desired, adjust the temperature.
5. Once the frozen drink reaches the optimal temperature, the unit will beep.
6. Enjoy immediately.

Orange Soda Slushi

Servings: 8

Ingredients:

5 (12-ounce) cans orange soda

⅓ cup white sugar

Preparation:

1. Put the orange soda and sugar into a large-sized pitcher and whisk to dissolve the sugar.
2. Pour the mixture into the vessel of Ninja Slushi.
3. Select "SLUSH". The preset will start at the default/optimal temperature for ideal texture.
4. If desired, adjust the temperature.
5. Once the frozen drink reaches the optimal temperature, the unit will beep.
6. Enjoy immediately.

Root Beer Soda Slushi

Servings: 8

Ingredients:

5 (12-ounce) cans root beer

⅓ cup white sugar

Preparation:

1. Put the root beer and sugar into a large-sized pitcher and whisk to dissolve the sugar.
2. Pour the mixture into the vessel of Ninja Slushi.
3. Select "SLUSH". The preset will start at the default/optimal temperature for ideal texture.
4. If desired, adjust the temperature.
5. Once the frozen drink reaches the optimal temperature, the unit will beep.
6. Enjoy immediately.

Grape Soda Slushi

Servings: 8

Ingredients:

5 (12-ounce) cans grape soda

⅓ cup white sugar

Preparation:

1. Put the grape soda and sugar into a large-sized pitcher and whisk to dissolve the sugar.
2. Pour the mixture into the vessel of Ninja Slushi.
3. Select "SLUSH". The preset will start at the default/optimal temperature for ideal texture.
4. If desired, adjust the temperature.
5. Once the frozen drink reaches the optimal temperature, the unit will beep.
6. Enjoy immediately.

Lemon Cola Soda Slushi

Servings: 8

Ingredients:

5 (12-ounce) cans cola soda
½ cup white sugar

⅓ cup lemon juice

Preparation:

1. Put all ingredients into a large-sized pitcher and whisk to dissolve the sugar.
2. Pour the mixture into the vessel of Ninja Slushi.
3. Select "SLUSH". The preset will start at the default/optimal temperature for ideal texture.
4. If desired, adjust the temperature.
5. Once the frozen drink reaches the optimal temperature, the unit will beep.
6. Enjoy immediately.

Lemon Probiotic Soda Slushi

Servings: 8

Ingredients:

5 (12-oz) cans flavored probiotic soda
½ cup white sugar

⅓ cup lemon juice

Preparation:

1. Put all ingredients into a large-sized pitcher and whisk to dissolve the sugar.
2. Pour the mixture into the vessel of Ninja Slushi.
3. Select "SLUSH". The preset will start at the default/optimal temperature for ideal texture.
4. If desired, adjust the temperature.
5. Once the frozen drink reaches the optimal temperature, the unit will beep.
6. Enjoy immediately.

Lime Cherry Cola Soda Slushi

Servings: 8

Ingredients:

5 (12-ounce) cans cherry cola soda

⅓ cup lime juice

⅓ cup white sugar

Preparation:

1. Put all ingredients into a large-sized pitcher and whisk to dissolve sugar.
2. Pour the mixture into the vessel of Ninja Slushi.
3. Select "SLUSH". The preset will start at the default/optimal temperature for ideal texture.
4. If desired, adjust the temperature.
5. Once the frozen drink reaches the optimal temperature, the unit will beep.
6. Enjoy immediately.

Apricot Soda Slushi

Servings: 8

Ingredients:

5 (12-ounce) cans soda

⅓ cup apricot juice

⅓ cup white sugar

Preparation:

1. Put all ingredients into a large-sized pitcher and whisk to dissolve sugar.
2. Pour the mixture into the vessel of Ninja Slushi.
3. Select "SLUSH". The preset will start at the default/optimal temperature for ideal texture.
4. If desired, adjust the temperature.
5. Once the frozen drink reaches the optimal temperature, the unit will beep.
6. Enjoy immediately.

Sweet Pomegranate Soda Slushi

Servings: 8

Ingredients:

5 (12-ounce) cans pomegranate soda

⅓ cup white sugar

Preparation:

1. Put the pomegranate soda and sugar into a large-sized pitcher and whisk to dissolve sugar.
2. Pour the mixture into the vessel of Ninja Slushi.
3. Select "SLUSH". The preset will start at the default/optimal temperature for ideal texture.
4. If desired, adjust the temperature.
5. Once the frozen drink reaches the optimal temperature, the unit will beep.
6. Enjoy immediately.

Lime Cola Soda Slushi

Servings: 8

Ingredients:

5 (12-ounce) cans cola soda
½ cup white sugar

⅓ cup lime juice

Preparation:

1. Put all ingredients into a large-sized pitcher and whisk to dissolve sugar.
2. Pour the mixture into the vessel of Ninja Slushi.
3. Select "SLUSH". The preset will start at the default/optimal temperature for ideal texture.
4. If desired, adjust the temperature.
5. Once the frozen drink reaches the optimal temperature, the unit will beep.
6. Enjoy immediately.

Grapefruit Soda Slushi

Ingredients:

5 (12-ounce) cans grapefruit soda   ⅓ cup white sugar

Preparation:

1. Put the grapefruit soda and sugar into a large-sized pitcher and whisk to dissolve sugar.
2. Pour the mixture into the vessel of Ninja Slushi.
3. Select "SLUSH". The preset will start at the default/optimal temperature for ideal texture.
4. If desired, adjust the temperature.
5. Once the frozen drink reaches the optimal temperature, the unit will beep.
6. Enjoy immediately.

Blackberry Soda Slushi

Servings: 8

Ingredients:

5 (12-ounce) cans blackberry soda   ⅓ cup white sugar

Preparation:

1. Put the blackberry soda and sugar into a large-sized pitcher and whisk to dissolve sugar.
2. Pour the mixture into the vessel of Ninja Slushi.
3. Select "SLUSH". The preset will start at the default/optimal temperature for ideal texture.
4. If desired, adjust the temperature.
5. Once the frozen drink reaches the optimal temperature, the unit will beep.
6. Enjoy immediately.

Chocolate Soda Slushi

Servings: 8

Ingredients:

5 (12-ounce) cans chocolate soda   ⅓ cup white sugar

Preparation:

1. Put the chocolate soda and sugar into a large-sized pitcher and whisk to dissolve sugar.
2. Pour the mixture into the vessel of Ninja Slushi.
3. Select "SLUSH". The preset will start at the default/optimal temperature for ideal texture.
4. If desired, adjust the temperature.
5. Once the frozen drink reaches the optimal temperature, the unit will beep.
6. Enjoy immediately.

Apple Beer Slushi

Servings: 8

Ingredients:

5 (12-ounce) cans apple beer   ⅓ cup white sugar

Preparation:

1. Put the apple beer and sugar into a large-sized pitcher and whisk to dissolve sugar.
2. Pour the mixture into the vessel of Ninja Slushi.
3. Select "SLUSH". The preset will start at the default/optimal temperature for ideal texture.
4. If desired, adjust the temperature.
5. Once the frozen drink reaches the optimal temperature, the unit will beep.
6. Enjoy immediately.

Red Cream Soda Slushi

Servings: 8

Ingredients:

5 (12-ounce) cans red cream soda   ⅓ cup white sugar

Preparation:

1. Put the red cream soda and sugar into a large-sized pitcher and whisk to dissolve sugar.
2. Pour the mixture into the vessel of Ninja Slushi.
3. Select "SLUSH". The preset will start at the default/optimal temperature for ideal texture.
4. If desired, adjust the temperature.
5. Once the frozen drink reaches the optimal temperature, the unit will beep.
6. Enjoy immediately.

Cranberry Soda Slushi

Servings: 8

Ingredients:

5 (12-ounce) cans cranberry soda   ⅓ cup white sugar

Preparation:

1. Put the cranberry soda and sugar into a large-sized pitcher and whisk to dissolve sugar.
2. Pour the mixture into the vessel of Ninja Slushi.
3. Select "SLUSH". The preset will start at the default/optimal temperature for ideal texture.
4. If desired, adjust the temperature.
5. Once the frozen drink reaches the optimal temperature, the unit will beep.
6. Enjoy immediately.

Chapter 4 Tea-Based Slushi Recipes

Sweet Tea Slushi... 47

Green Tea Slushi 47

Matcha Tea Slushi 48

Chai Tea Slushi 48

Limeade Iced Tea Slushi 49

Lemonade Iced Tea Slushi................................... 49

Strawberry Iced Tea Slushi 50

Pomegranate Iced Tea Slushi 50

Mango Iced Tea Slushi 51

Peach Iced Tea Slushi 51

Raspberry Iced Tea Slushi.................................. 52

Apple Iced Tea Slushi 52

Fresh Peach Iced Tea Slushi 53

Lemon Iced Tea Slushi 53

Blueberry Iced Tea Slushi 54

Cherry Iced Tea Slushi 54

Lime Green Tea Slushi 55

Lemon Matcha Tea Slushi.................................. 55

Cranberry Iced Tea Slushi 56

Tropical Fruit Iced Tea Slushi 56

Sweet Tea Slushi

Ingredients:

8 cups chilled sweetened tea   ⅓ cup white sugar

Preparation:

1. Put the tea and sugar into a large-sized pitcher and whisk to dissolve the sugar.
2. Pour the mixture into the vessel of Ninja Slushi.
3. Select "SLUSH". The preset will start at the default/optimal temperature for ideal texture.
4. If desired, adjust the temperature.
5. Once the frozen drink reaches the optimal temperature, the unit will beep.
6. Enjoy immediately.

Green Tea Slushi

Servings: 8

Ingredients:

8 cups chilled sweetened green tea   ⅓ cup white sugar

Preparation:

1. Put the green tea and sugar into a large-sized pitcher and whisk to dissolve the sugar.
2. Pour the mixture into the vessel of Ninja Slushi.
3. Select "SLUSH". The preset will start at the default/optimal temperature for ideal texture.
4. If desired, adjust the temperature.
5. Once the frozen drink reaches the optimal temperature, the unit will beep.
6. Enjoy immediately.

Matcha Tea Slushi

Servings: 8

Ingredients:

8 cups chilled sweetened matcha tea   ⅓ cup white sugar

Preparation:

1. Put the matcha tea and sugar into a large-sized pitcher and whisk to dissolve the sugar.
2. Pour the mixture into the vessel of Ninja Slushi.
3. Select "SLUSH". The preset will start at the default/optimal temperature for ideal texture.
4. If desired, adjust the temperature.
5. Once the frozen drink reaches the optimal temperature, the unit will beep.
6. Enjoy immediately.

Chai Tea Slushi

Servings: 8

Ingredients:

8 cups chilled sweetened chai tea   ⅓ cup white sugar

Preparation:

1. Put the chai tea and sugar into a large-sized pitcher and whisk to dissolve the sugar.
2. Pour the mixture into the vessel of Ninja Slushi.
3. Select "SLUSH". The preset will start at the default/optimal temperature for ideal texture.
4. If desired, adjust the temperature.
5. Once the frozen drink reaches the optimal temperature, the unit will beep.
6. Enjoy immediately.

Limeade Iced Tea Slushi

Servings: 8

Ingredients:

5 cups sweetened limeade
2¾ cups sweetened iced tea

¼ cup white sugar

Preparation:

1. Put all ingredients into a large-sized pitcher and whisk to dissolve the sugar.
2. Pour the mixture into the vessel of Ninja Slushi.
3. Select "SLUSH". The preset will start at the default/optimal temperature for ideal texture.
4. If desired, adjust the temperature.
5. Once the frozen drink reaches the optimal temperature, the unit will beep.
6. Enjoy immediately.

Lemonade Iced Tea Slushi

Servings: 8

Ingredients:

5 cups sweetened lemonade
2¾ cups sweetened iced tea

¼ cup white sugar

Preparation:

1. Put all ingredients into a large-sized pitcher and whisk to dissolve the sugar.
2. Pour the mixture into the vessel of Ninja Slushi.
3. Select "SLUSH". The preset will start at the default/optimal temperature for ideal texture.
4. If desired, adjust the temperature.
5. Once the frozen drink reaches the optimal temperature, the unit will beep.
6. Enjoy immediately.

Strawberry Iced Tea Slushi

Servings: 8

Ingredients:

5 cups sweetened iced tea
2¾ cups strawberry juice

¼ cup white sugar

Preparation:

1. Put all ingredients into a large-sized pitcher and whisk to dissolve the sugar.
2. Pour the mixture into the vessel of Ninja Slushi.
3. Select "SLUSH". The preset will start at the default/optimal temperature for ideal texture.
4. If desired, adjust the temperature.
5. Once the frozen drink reaches the optimal temperature, the unit will beep.
6. Enjoy immediately.

Pomegranate Iced Tea Slushi

Servings: 8

Ingredients:

5 cups sweetened iced tea
2¾ cups pomegranate juice

¼ cup white sugar

Preparation:

1. Put all ingredients into a large-sized pitcher and whisk to dissolve the sugar.
2. Pour the mixture into the vessel of Ninja Slushi.
3. Select "SLUSH". The preset will start at the default/optimal temperature for ideal texture.
4. If desired, adjust the temperature.
5. Once the frozen drink reaches the optimal temperature, the unit will beep.
6. Enjoy immediately.

Mango Iced Tea Slushi

Ingredients:

5 cups sweetened iced tea
2¾ cups mango nectar

¼ cup white sugar

Preparation:

1. Put all ingredients into a large-sized pitcher and whisk to dissolve the sugar.
2. Pour the mixture into the vessel of Ninja Slushi.
3. Select "SLUSH". The preset will start at the default/optimal temperature for ideal texture.
4. If desired, adjust the temperature.
5. Once the frozen drink reaches the optimal temperature, the unit will beep.
6. Enjoy immediately.

Peach Iced Tea Slushi

Servings: 8

Ingredients:

5 cups sweetened iced tea
2¾ cups peach nectar

¼ cup white sugar

Preparation:

1. Put all ingredients into a large-sized pitcher and whisk to dissolve the sugar.
2. Pour the mixture into the vessel of Ninja Slushi.
3. Select "SLUSH". The preset will start at the default/optimal temperature for ideal texture.
4. If desired, adjust the temperature.
5. Once the frozen drink reaches the optimal temperature, the unit will beep.
6. Enjoy immediately.

Raspberry Iced Tea Slushi

Servings: 8

Ingredients:

8 cups raspberry iced tea

⅓ cup white sugar

Preparation:

1. Put the raspberry iced tea and sugar into a large-sized pitcher and whisk to dissolve the sugar.
2. Pour the mixture into the vessel of Ninja Slushi.
3. Select "SLUSH". The preset will start at the default/optimal temperature for ideal texture.
4. If desired, adjust the temperature.
5. Once the frozen drink reaches the optimal temperature, the unit will beep.
6. Enjoy immediately.

Apple Iced Tea Slushi

Servings: 8

Ingredients:

5 cups sweetened iced tea
2¾ cups apple juice

¼ cup white sugar

Preparation:

1. Put all ingredients into a large-sized pitcher and whisk to dissolve the sugar.
2. Pour the mixture into the vessel of Ninja Slushi.
3. Select "SLUSH". The preset will start at the default/optimal temperature for ideal texture.
4. If desired, adjust the temperature.
5. Once the frozen drink reaches the optimal temperature, the unit will beep.
6. Enjoy immediately.

Fresh Peach Iced Tea Slushi

Servings: 8

Ingredients:

5 cups sweetened iced tea

2¾ cups peach juice

¼ cup white sugar

Preparation:

1. Put all ingredients into a large-sized pitcher and whisk to dissolve the sugar.
2. Pour the mixture into the vessel of Ninja Slushi.
3. Select "SLUSH". The preset will start at the default/optimal temperature for ideal texture.
4. If desired, adjust the temperature.
5. Once the frozen drink reaches the optimal temperature, the unit will beep.
6. Enjoy immediately.

Lemon Iced Tea Slushi

Servings: 8

Ingredients:

8 cups lemon iced tea

⅓ cup white sugar

Preparation:

1. Put the tea and sugar into a large-sized pitcher and whisk to dissolve the sugar.
2. Pour the mixture into the vessel of Ninja Slushi.
3. Select "SLUSH". The preset will start at the default/optimal temperature for ideal texture.
4. If desired, adjust the temperature.
5. Once the frozen drink reaches the optimal temperature, the unit will beep.
6. Enjoy immediately.

Blueberry Iced Tea Slushi

Servings: 8

Ingredients:

5 cups sweetened iced tea   ¼ cup white sugar
2¾ cups blueberry nectar

Preparation:

1. Put all ingredients into a large-sized pitcher and whisk to dissolve the sugar.
2. Pour the mixture into the vessel of Ninja Slushi.
3. Select "SLUSH". The preset will start at the default/optimal temperature for ideal texture.
4. If desired, adjust the temperature.
5. Once the frozen drink reaches the optimal temperature, the unit will beep.
6. Enjoy immediately.

Cherry Iced Tea Slushi

Servings: 8

Ingredients:

5 cups sweetened iced tea   ¼ cup white sugar
2¾ cups cherry nectar

Preparation:

1. Put all ingredients into a large-sized pitcher and whisk to dissolve the sugar.
2. Pour the mixture into the vessel of Ninja Slushi.
3. Select "SLUSH". The preset will start at the default/optimal temperature for ideal texture.
4. If desired, adjust the temperature.
5. Once the frozen drink reaches the optimal temperature, the unit will beep.
6. Enjoy immediately.

Lime Green Tea Slushi

Ingredients:

5 cups sweetened limeade
2¾ cups chilled green tea

¼ cup white sugar

Preparation:

1. Put all ingredients into a large-sized pitcher and whisk to dissolve the sugar.
2. Pour the mixture into the vessel of Ninja Slushi.
3. Select "SLUSH". The preset will start at the default/optimal temperature for ideal texture.
4. If desired, adjust the temperature.
5. Once the frozen drink reaches the optimal temperature, the unit will beep.
6. Enjoy immediately.

Lemon Matcha Tea Slushi

Servings: 8

Ingredients:

5 cups sweetened lemonade
2¾ cups chilled matcha tea

¼ cup white sugar

Preparation:

1. Put all ingredients into a large-sized pitcher and whisk to dissolve the sugar.
2. Pour the mixture into the vessel of Ninja Slushi.
3. Select "SLUSH". The preset will start at the default/optimal temperature for ideal texture.
4. If desired, adjust the temperature.
5. Once the frozen drink reaches the optimal temperature, the unit will beep.
6. Enjoy immediately.

Cranberry Iced Tea Slushi

Servings: 8

Ingredients:

5 cups sweetened iced tea
2¾ cups cranberry juice

¼ cup white sugar

Preparation:

1. Put all ingredients into a large-sized pitcher and whisk to dissolve the sugar.
2. Pour the mixture into the vessel of Ninja Slushi.
3. Select "SLUSH". The preset will start at the default/optimal temperature for ideal texture.
4. If desired, adjust the temperature.
5. Once the frozen drink reaches the optimal temperature, the unit will beep.
6. Enjoy immediately.

Tropical Fruit Iced Tea Slushi

Servings: 8

Ingredients:

5 cups sweetened iced tea
2¾ cups tropical fruit nectar

¼ cup white sugar

Preparation:

1. Put all ingredients into a large-sized pitcher and whisk to dissolve the sugar.
2. Pour the mixture into the vessel of Ninja Slushi.
3. Select "SLUSH". The preset will start at the default/optimal temperature for ideal texture.
4. If desired, adjust the temperature.
5. Once the frozen drink reaches the optimal temperature, the unit will beep.
6. Enjoy immediately.

Chapter 5 Spiked Slushi Recipes

Rosé Wine Spiked Slushi …………………………… 58

Orange Red Wine Spiked Slushi …………………… 58

Peach Champagne Spiked Slushi ………………… 59

Tasty Espresso Martini Spiked Slushi …………… 59

Homemade Orange Spritz Spiked Slushi………… 60

Fruity Rum Spiked Slushi………………………… 60

Pineapple-Orange Rum Spiked Slushi …………… 61

Cream Mocha Spiked Slushi……………………… 61

Apple Cider Whiskey Spiked Slushi ……………… 62

Coconut Limeade Spiked Slushi ………………… 62

Mango Daiquiri Spiked Slushi …………………… 63

Strawberry Margarita Spiked Slushi …………… 63

Strawberry Rosé Wine Spiked Slushi …………… 64

Hard Kombucha Spiked Slushi …………………… 64

Champagne Mango Spiked Slushi ……………… 65

White Wine Spiked Slushi………………………… 65

Cranberry Rosé Wine Spiked Slushi …………… 66

Coconut Pineapple Rum Spiked Slushi ………… 66

Orange Mango Rum Spiked Slushi ……………… 67

Chocolate Caramel Spiked Slushi………………… 67

Rosé Wine Spiked Slushi

Servings: 8

Ingredients:

7½ cups rosé wine

⅓ cup white sugar

Preparation:

1. Put the rose wine and sugar into a large-sized pitcher and whisk to dissolve the sugar.
2. Pour the mixture into the vessel of Ninja Slushi.
3. Select "SPIKED SLUSH". The preset will start at the default/optimal temperature for ideal texture.
4. If desired, adjust the temperature.
5. Once the frozen drink reaches the optimal temperature, the unit will beep.
6. Enjoy immediately.

Orange Red Wine Spiked Slushi

Servings: 8

Ingredients:

3¼ cups red wine
½ cup orange liqueur

3¾ cups orange juice
¼ cup light brown sugar

Preparation:

1. Put all ingredients into a large-sized pitcher and whisk to dissolve the sugar.
2. Pour the mixture into the vessel of Ninja Slushi.
3. Select "SPIKED SLUSH". The preset will start at the default/optimal temperature for ideal texture.
4. If desired, adjust the temperature.
5. Once the frozen drink reaches the optimal temperature, the unit will beep.
6. Enjoy immediately.

Peach Champagne Spiked Slushi

Servings: 8

Ingredients:

6⅔ cups peach nectar

1¼ cups champagne

¼ cup white sugar

Preparation:

1. Put all ingredients into a large-sized pitcher and whisk to dissolve the sugar.
2. Pour the mixture into the vessel of Ninja Slushi.
3. Select "SPIKED SLUSH". The preset will start at the default/optimal temperature for ideal texture.
4. If desired, adjust the temperature.
5. Once the frozen drink reaches the optimal temperature, the unit will beep.
6. Enjoy immediately.

Tasty Espresso Martini Spiked Slushi

Servings: 8

Ingredients:

½ cup plus 2 tablespoons vodka

⅓ cup coffee liquor

⅓ cup Irish cream

4 cups cold brew coffee

2¾ cups water

¼ cup white sugar

Preparation:

1. Put all ingredients into a large-sized pitcher and whisk to dissolve the sugar.
2. Pour the mixture into the vessel of Ninja Slushi.
3. Select "SPIKED SLUSH". The preset will start at the default/optimal temperature for ideal texture.
4. If desired, adjust the temperature.
5. Once the frozen drink reaches the optimal temperature, the unit will beep.
6. Enjoy immediately.

Homemade Orange Spritz Spiked Slushi

Ingredients:

2 cups Italian orange aperitivo

⅔ cup nectarine juice

4 cups dry prosecco

1⅓ cups water

¼ cup white sugar

Preparation:

1. Put all ingredients into a large-sized pitcher and whisk to dissolve the sugar.
2. Pour the mixture into the vessel of Ninja Slushi.
3. Select "SPIKED SLUSH". The preset will start at the default/optimal temperature for ideal texture.
4. If desired, adjust the temperature.
5. Once the frozen drink reaches the optimal temperature, the unit will beep.
6. Enjoy immediately.

Fruity Rum Spiked Slushi

Servings: 8

Ingredients:

⅓ cup dark rum

⅓ cup light rum

⅓ cup banana liquor

⅓ cup blackberry brandy

⅓ cup grenadine

2⅓ cups pineapple juice

2⅔ cups orange juice

1⅓ cups water

¼ cup white sugar

Preparation:

1. Put all ingredients into a large-sized pitcher and whisk to dissolve the sugar.
2. Pour the mixture into the vessel of Ninja Slushi.
3. Select "SPIKED SLUSH". The preset will start at the default/optimal temperature for ideal texture.
4. If desired, adjust the temperature.
5. Once the frozen drink reaches the optimal temperature, the unit will beep.
6. Enjoy immediately.

Pineapple-Orange Rum Spiked Slushi

Servings: 8

Ingredients:

⅓ cup dark rum

⅓ cup coconut rum

2⅔ cups pineapple juice

2⅔ cups orange juice

1⅓ cups water

¼ cup plus 2 tablespoons lime juice

¼ cup white sugar

Preparation:

1. Put all ingredients into a large-sized pitcher and whisk to dissolve the sugar.
2. Pour the mixture into the vessel of Ninja Slushi.
3. Select "SPIKED SLUSH". The preset will start at the default/optimal temperature for ideal texture.
4. If desired, adjust the temperature.
5. Once the frozen drink reaches the optimal temperature, the unit will beep.
6. Enjoy immediately.

Cream Mocha Spiked Slushi

Servings: 8

Ingredients:

4 cups whole milk

1⅓ cups heavy cream

1⅓ cups chocolate syrup

½ cup vodka

½ cup coffee liquor

⅓ cup Irish cream

¼ cup white sugar

Preparation:

1. Put all ingredients into a large-sized pitcher and whisk to dissolve the sugar.
2. Pour the mixture into the vessel of Ninja Slushi.
3. Select "SPIKED SLUSH". The preset will start at the default/optimal temperature for ideal texture.
4. If desired, adjust the temperature.
5. Once the frozen drink reaches the optimal temperature, the unit will beep.
6. Enjoy immediately.

Apple Cider Whiskey Spiked Slushi

Servings: 8

Ingredients:

6⅔ cups apple cider

1¼ cups cinnamon whiskey

¼ cup white sugar

Preparation:

1. Put all ingredients into a large-sized pitcher and whisk to dissolve the sugar.
2. Pour the mixture into the vessel of Ninja Slushi.
3. Select "SPIKED SLUSH". The preset will start at the default/optimal temperature for ideal texture.
4. If desired, adjust the temperature.
5. Once the frozen drink reaches the optimal temperature, the unit will beep.
6. Enjoy immediately.

Coconut Limeade Spiked Slushi

Servings: 8

Ingredients:

3⅓ cups unsweetened canned coconut milk

3⅓ cups sweetened limeade

1 cup light rum

¼ cup lime juice

¼ cup white sugar

Preparation:

1. Put all ingredients into a large-sized pitcher and whisk to dissolve the sugar.
2. Pour the mixture into the vessel of Ninja Slushi.
3. Select "SPIKED SLUSH". The preset will start at the default/optimal temperature for ideal texture.
4. If desired, adjust the temperature.
5. Once the frozen drink reaches the optimal temperature, the unit will beep.
6. Enjoy immediately.

Mango Daiquiri Spiked Slushi

Servings: 8

Ingredients:

3¼ cups lite mango daiquiri drink mix

2¼ cups water

½ cup white rum

⅓ cup white sugar

Preparation:

1. Put all ingredients into a large-sized pitcher and whisk to dissolve the sugar.
2. Pour the mixture into the vessel of Ninja Slushi.
3. Select "SPIKED SLUSH". The preset will start at the default/optimal temperature for ideal texture.
4. If desired, adjust the temperature.
5. Once the frozen drink reaches the optimal temperature, the unit will beep.
6. Enjoy immediately.

Strawberry Margarita Spiked Slushi

Servings: 8

Ingredients:

3¼ cups strawberry margarita drink mix

2¼ cups water

½ cup tequila

⅓ cup white sugar

Preparation:

1. Put all ingredients into a large-sized pitcher and whisk to dissolve the sugar.
2. Pour the mixture into the vessel of Ninja Slushi.
3. Select "SPIKED SLUSH". The preset will start at the default/optimal temperature for ideal texture.
4. If desired, adjust the temperature.
5. Once the frozen drink reaches the optimal temperature, the unit will beep.
6. Enjoy immediately.

Strawberry Rosé Wine Spiked Slushi

Ingredients:

5 cups dry rosé wine

1¼ cups strawberry seltzer water

⅔ cup simple syrup

⅔ cup lemon juice

Preparation:

1. Put all ingredients into a large-sized pitcher and whisk to incorporate.
2. Pour the mixture into the vessel of Ninja Slushi.
3. Select "SPIKED SLUSH". The preset will start at the default/optimal temperature for ideal texture.
4. If desired, adjust the temperature.
5. Once the frozen drink reaches the optimal temperature, the unit will beep.
6. Enjoy immediately.

Hard Kombucha Spiked Slushi

Servings: 8

Ingredients:

7½ cups hard kombucha (grapefruit flavored)

⅓ cup white sugar

Preparation:

1. Put the kombucha and sugar into a large-sized pitcher and whisk to dissolve the sugar.
2. Pour the mixture into the vessel of Ninja Slushi.
3. Select "SPIKED SLUSH". The preset will start at the default/optimal temperature for ideal texture.
4. If desired, adjust the temperature.
5. Once the frozen drink reaches the optimal temperature, the unit will beep.
6. Enjoy immediately.

Champagne Mango Spiked Slushi

Ingredients:

6⅔ cups mango nectar   ¼ cup white sugar

1¼ cups champagne

Preparation:

1. Put all ingredients into a large-sized pitcher and whisk to dissolve the sugar.

2. Pour the mixture into the vessel of Ninja Slushi.

3. Select "SPIKED SLUSH". The preset will start at the default/optimal temperature for ideal texture.

4. If desired, adjust the temperature.

5. Once the frozen drink reaches the optimal temperature, the unit will beep.

6. Enjoy immediately.

White Wine Spiked Slushi

Servings: 8

Ingredients:

7½ cups white wine   ⅓ cup white sugar

Preparation:

1. Put the wine and sugar into a large-sized pitcher and whisk to dissolve the sugar.

2. Pour the mixture into the vessel of Ninja Slushi.

3. Select "SPIKED SLUSH". The preset will start at the default/optimal temperature for ideal texture.

4. If desired, adjust the temperature.

5. Once the frozen drink reaches the optimal temperature, the unit will beep.

6. Enjoy immediately.

Cranberry Rosé Wine Spiked Slushi

Servings: 8

Ingredients:

4⅓ cups rosé wine
3 cups white cranberry juice

⅔ cup simple syrup

Preparation:

1. Put all ingredients into a large-sized pitcher and whisk to incorporate.
2. Pour the mixture into the vessel of Ninja Slushi.
3. Select "SPIKED SLUSH". The preset will start at the default/optimal temperature for ideal texture.
4. If desired, adjust the temperature.
5. Once the frozen drink reaches the optimal temperature, the unit will beep.
6. Enjoy immediately.

Coconut Pineapple Rum Spiked Slushi

Servings: 8

Ingredients:

4⅓ cups pineapple juice
⅔ cup simple syrup

1¼ cups spiced rum
1¼ cups canned full-fat coconut milk

Preparation:

1. Put all ingredients into a large-sized pitcher and whisk to incorporate.
2. Pour the mixture into the vessel of Ninja Slushi.
3. Select "SPIKED SLUSH". The preset will start at the default/optimal temperature for ideal texture.
4. If desired, adjust the temperature.
5. Once the frozen drink reaches the optimal temperature, the unit will beep.
6. Enjoy immediately.

Orange Mango Rum Spiked Slushi

Servings: 8

Ingredients:

4 cups mango juice

⅔ cup dark rum

1⅓ cups coconut milk

1⅓ cups orange juice

⅔ cup water

⅓ cup white sugar

Preparation:

1. Put all ingredients into a large-sized pitcher and whisk to dissolve the sugar.
2. Pour the mixture into the vessel of Ninja Slushi.
3. Select "SPIKED SLUSH". The preset will start at the default/optimal temperature for ideal texture.
4. If desired, adjust the temperature.
5. Once the frozen drink reaches the optimal temperature, the unit will beep.
6. Enjoy immediately.

Chocolate Caramel Spiked Slushi

Servings: 8

Ingredients:

4 cups whole milk

1⅓ cups heavy cream

1⅓ cups chocolate syrup

½ cup vodka

½ cup chocolate caramel liquor

⅓ cup Irish cream

¼ cup white sugar

Preparation:

1. Put all ingredients into a large-sized pitcher and whisk to dissolve the sugar.
2. Pour the mixture into the vessel of Ninja Slushi.
3. Select "SPIKED SLUSH". The preset will start at the default/optimal temperature for ideal texture.
4. If desired, adjust the temperature.
5. Once the frozen drink reaches the optimal temperature, the unit will beep.
6. Enjoy immediately.

Chapter 6 Sugar-Free Slushi Recipes

Limeade Slushi 69

Lemon Strawberry Seltzer Slushi...................... 69

Mixed Fruit Sports Drink Slushi 70

Lime Seltzer Slushi 70

Pink Lemonade Slushi 71

Vanilla Milkshake 71

Cranberry-Grape Frozen Juice Slushi 72

Easy Margarita Spiked Slushi 72

Strawberry Daiquiri Spiked Slushi 73

Cranberry Vodka Spiked Slushi 73

Strawberry Lemonade Slushi 74

Raspberry Lemonade Slushi........................... 74

Cherry Lime Slushi 75

Cherry Slushi 75

Cranberry Apple Slushi................................. 76

Tasty Orange Frozen Juice Slushi..................... 76

Apple Frozen Juice Slushi 77

Lime Daiquiri Spiked Slushi 77

Orange Prosecco Spiked Slushi........................ 78

Coconut Lemonade Spiked Slushi 78

Limeade Slushi

Ingredients:

7½ cups sugar-free limeade

½ cup liquid allulose

Preparation:

1. Put all ingredients into a large-sized pitcher and whisk to incorporate.
2. Pour the mixture into the vessel of Ninja Slushi.
3. Select "SLUSH". The preset will start at the default/optimal temperature for ideal texture.
4. If desired, adjust the temperature.
5. Once the frozen drink reaches the optimal temperature, the unit will beep.
6. Enjoy immediately.

Lemon Strawberry Seltzer Slushi

Servings: 8

Ingredients:

5 (12-ounce) cans strawberry seltzer water
½ cup liquid allulose

⅓ cup lemon juice

Preparation:

1. Put all ingredients into a large-sized pitcher and whisk to incorporate.
2. Pour the mixture into the vessel of Ninja Slushi.
3. Select "SLUSH". The preset will start at the default/optimal temperature for ideal texture.
4. If desired, adjust the temperature.
5. Once the frozen drink reaches the optimal temperature, the unit will beep.
6. Enjoy immediately.

Mixed Fruit Sports Drink Slushi

Servings: 8

Ingredients:

7½ cups sugar-free mixed fruit sports drink   ½ cup liquid allulose

Preparation:

1. Put all ingredients into a large-sized pitcher and whisk to incorporate.
2. Pour the mixture into the vessel of Ninja Slushi.
3. Select "SLUSH". The preset will start at the default/optimal temperature for ideal texture.
4. If desired, adjust the temperature.
5. Once the frozen drink reaches the optimal temperature, the unit will beep.
6. Enjoy immediately.

Lime Seltzer Slushi

Servings: 8

Ingredients:

8 cups lime seltzer water   ½ cup liquid allulose

Preparation:

1. Put all ingredients into a large-sized pitcher and whisk to incorporate.
2. Pour the mixture into the vessel of Ninja Slushi.
3. Select "SLUSH". The preset will start at the default/optimal temperature for ideal texture.
4. If desired, adjust the temperature.
5. Once the frozen drink reaches the optimal temperature, the unit will beep.
6. Enjoy immediately.

Pink Lemonade Slushi

Ingredients:

7⅓ cups water

¾ cup plus 2 tablespoons sugar-free pink lemonade powder mix

½ cup liquid allulose

Preparation:

1. Put all ingredients into a large-sized pitcher and whisk to incorporate.
2. Pour the mixture into the vessel of Ninja Slushi.
3. Select "SLUSH". The preset will start at the default/optimal temperature for ideal texture.
4. If desired, adjust the temperature.
5. Once the frozen drink reaches the optimal temperature, the unit will beep.
6. Enjoy immediately.

Vanilla Milkshake

Ingredients:

6⅔ cups whole milk

1⅓ cups heavy cream

½ cup liquid allulose

3 tablespoons vanilla extract

Preparation:

1. Put all ingredients into a large-sized pitcher and whisk to dissolve the sugar.
2. Pour the mixture into the vessel of Ninja Slushi.
3. Select "MILKSHAKE". The preset will start at the default/optimal temperature for ideal texture.
4. If desired, adjust the temperature.
5. Once the frozen drink reaches the optimal temperature, the unit will beep.
6. Enjoy immediately.

Cranberry-Grape Frozen Juice Slushi

Ingredients:

8 cups sugar-free cranberry grape juice

½ cup liquid allulose

Preparation:

1. Put all ingredients into a large-sized pitcher and whisk to incorporate.
2. Pour the mixture into the vessel of Ninja Slushi.
3. Select "FROZEN JUICE". The preset will start at the default temperature for ideal texture.
4. If desired, adjust the temperature.
5. Once the frozen drink reaches the optimal temperature, the unit will beep.
6. Enjoy immediately.

Easy Margarita Spiked Slushi

Ingredients:

3¼ cups sugar free margarita drink mix
2¼ cups water

½ cup tequila
½ cup liquid allulose

Preparation:

1. Put all ingredients into a large-sized pitcher and whisk to incorporate.
2. Pour the mixture into the vessel of Ninja Slushi.
3. Select "SPIKED SLUSH". The preset will start at the default/optimal temperature for ideal texture.
4. If desired, adjust the temperature.
5. Once the frozen drink reaches the optimal temperature, the unit will beep.
6. Enjoy immediately.

Strawberry Daiquiri Spiked Slushi

Servings: 8

Ingredients:

3¼ cups sugar-free strawberry daiquiri mix

2¼ plus 2 tablespoons water

½ cup white rum

½ cup liquid allulose

Preparation:

1. Put all ingredients into a large-sized pitcher and whisk to incorporate.
2. Pour the mixture into the vessel of Ninja Slushi.
3. Select "SPIKED SLUSH". The preset will start at the default/optimal temperature for ideal texture.
4. If desired, adjust the temperature.
5. Once the frozen drink reaches the optimal temperature, the unit will beep.
6. Enjoy immediately.
7. Pour all ingredients into the vessel.

Cranberry Vodka Spiked Slushi

Servings: 8

Ingredients:

6⅔ cups unsweetened cranberry juice

1¼ cups vodka

⅓ cup liquid allulose

Preparation:

1. Put all ingredients into a large-sized pitcher and whisk to incorporate.
2. Pour the mixture into the vessel of Ninja Slushi.
3. Select "SPIKED SLUSH". The preset will start at the default/optimal temperature for ideal texture.
4. If desired, adjust the temperature.
5. Once the frozen drink reaches the optimal temperature, the unit will beep.
6. Enjoy immediately.

Strawberry Lemonade Slushi

Ingredients:

7⅓ cups water

¾ cup plus 2 tablespoons sugar-free strawberry

lemonade powder mix

½ cup liquid allulose

Preparation:

1. Put all ingredients into a large-sized pitcher and whisk to incorporate.
2. Pour the mixture into the vessel of Ninja Slushi.
3. Select "SLUSH". The preset will start at the default/optimal temperature for ideal texture.
4. If desired, adjust the temperature.
5. Once the frozen drink reaches the optimal temperature, the unit will beep.
6. Enjoy immediately.

Raspberry Lemonade Slushi

Servings: 8

Ingredients:

7½ cups unsweetened raspberry lemonade

½ cup liquid allulose

Preparation:

1. Put the raspberry lemonade and liquid allulose into a large-sized pitcher and whisk to incorporate.
2. Pour the mixture into the vessel of Ninja Slushi.
3. Select "SLUSH". The preset will start at the default/optimal temperature for ideal texture.
4. If desired, adjust the temperature.
5. Once the frozen drink reaches the optimal temperature, the unit will beep.
6. Enjoy immediately.

Cherry Lime Slushi

Servings: 8

Ingredients:

7½ cups sugar-free cherry lime sports drink   ½ cup liquid allulose

Preparation:

1. Put the cherry lime sports drink and liquid allulose into a large-sized pitcher and whisk to incorporate.
2. Pour the mixture into the vessel of Ninja Slushi.
3. Select "SLUSH". The preset will start at the default/optimal temperature for ideal texture.
4. If desired, adjust the temperature.
5. Once the frozen drink reaches the optimal temperature, the unit will beep.
6. Enjoy immediately.

Cherry Slushi

Servings: 8

Ingredients:

7½ cups unsweetened cherry juice   ½ cup liquid allulose

Preparation:

1. Put the cherry juice and liquid allulose into a large-sized pitcher and whisk to incorporate.
2. Pour the mixture into the vessel of Ninja Slushi.
3. Select "SLUSH". The preset will start at the default/optimal temperature for ideal texture.
4. If desired, adjust the temperature.
5. Once the frozen drink reaches the optimal temperature, the unit will beep.
6. Enjoy immediately.

Cranberry Apple Slushi

Servings: 8

Ingredients:

8 cups sugar-free cranberry apple drink   ½ cup liquid allulose

Preparation:

1. Put the cranberry apple drink and liquid allulose into a large-sized pitcher and whisk to incorporate.
2. Pour the mixture into the vessel of Ninja Slushi.
3. Select "SLUSH". The preset will start at the default/optimal temperature for ideal texture.
4. If desired, adjust the temperature.
5. Once the frozen drink reaches the optimal temperature, the unit will beep.
6. Enjoy immediately.

Tasty Orange Frozen Juice Slushi

Servings: 8

Ingredients:

8 cups unsweetened orange juice   ½ cup liquid allulose

Preparation:

1. Put the orange juice and liquid allulose into a large-sized pitcher and whisk to incorporate.
2. Pour the mixture into the vessel of Ninja Slushi.
3. Select "FROZEN JUICE". The preset will start at the default temperature for ideal texture.
4. If desired, adjust the temperature.
5. Once the frozen drink reaches the optimal temperature, the unit will beep.
6. Enjoy immediately.

Apple Frozen Juice Slushi

Servings: 8

Ingredients:

6 cups unsweetened apple juice

½ cup liquid allulose

Preparation:

1. Put the apple juice and liquid allulose into a large-sized pitcher and whisk to incorporate.
2. Pour the mixture into the vessel of Ninja Slushi.
3. Select "FROZEN JUICE". The preset will start at the default temperature for ideal texture.
4. If desired, adjust the temperature.
5. Once the frozen drink reaches the optimal temperature, the unit will beep.
6. Enjoy immediately.

Lime Daiquiri Spiked Slushi

Servings: 8

Ingredients:

3¼ cups sugar-free lime daiquiri mix
2¼ plus 2 tablespoons water

½ cup white rum
½ cup liquid allulose

Preparation:

1. Put all ingredients into a large-sized pitcher and whisk to incorporate.
2. Pour the mixture into the vessel of Ninja Slushi.
3. Select "SPIKED SLUSH". The preset will start at the default/optimal temperature for ideal texture.
4. If desired, adjust the temperature.
5. Once the frozen drink reaches the optimal temperature, the unit will beep.
6. Enjoy immediately.

Orange Prosecco Spiked Slushi

Servings: 8

Ingredients:

2 cups Italian orange aperitivo

⅔ cup unsweetened orange juice

4 cups dry prosecco

1⅓ cups water

½ cup liquid allulose

Preparation:

1. Put all ingredients into a large-sized pitcher and whisk to incorporate.
2. Pour the mixture into the vessel of Ninja Slushi.
3. Select "SPIKED SLUSH". The preset will start at the default/optimal temperature for ideal texture.
4. If desired, adjust the temperature.
5. Once the frozen drink reaches the optimal temperature, the unit will beep.
6. Enjoy immediately.

Coconut Lemonade Spiked Slushi

Servings: 8

Ingredients:

3⅓ cups unsweetened canned coconut milk

3⅓ cups unsweetened lemonade

1 cup light rum

¼ cup lemon juice

½ cup liquid allulose

Preparation:

1. Put all ingredients into a large-sized pitcher and whisk to incorporate.
2. Pour the mixture into the vessel of Ninja Slushi.
3. Select "SPIKED SLUSH". The preset will start at the default/optimal temperature for ideal texture.
4. If desired, adjust the temperature.
5. Once the frozen drink reaches the optimal temperature, the unit will beep.
6. Enjoy immediately.

Chapter 7 Frappé Recipes

Pumpkin Spice Frappé 80

Mocha Frappé 80

Vanilla Oat Frappé 81

Caramel Coffee Frappé 81

Sweet Oat Caramel Frappé 82

Coffee Frappé 82

Chocolate Frappé 83

Matcha Latte Frappé 83

Golden Milk Frappé 84

Hazelnut Latte Frappé 84

Vanilla Caramel Macchiato Frappé 85

Peppermint Mocha Frappé 85

French Vanilla Frappé 86

Cinnamon Coconut Frappé 86

Pumpkin Pie Latte Frappé 87

Vanilla Hazelnut Frappé 87

Chocolate Caramel Frappé 88

Vanilla Cinnamon Frappé 88

Strawberry Latte Frappé 89

Violet Latte Frappé 89

Pumpkin Spice Frappé

Servings: 8

Ingredients:

2¾ cups pumpkin spice creamer

3¼ cups black coffee

2 teaspoons vanilla extract

⅓ cup white sugar

Preparation:

1. Put all ingredients into a large-sized pitcher and whisk to dissolve the sugar.
2. Pour the mixture into the vessel of Ninja Slushi.
3. Select "FRAPPE". The preset will start at the default/optimal level.
4. Adjust the temperature control to illuminate 4 bars.
5. Once the frozen drink reaches the optimal temperature, the unit will beep.
6. Enjoy immediately with your favorite topping.

Mocha Frappé

Servings: 8

Ingredients:

2½ cups half-and-half

5 cups black coffee

1 cup mocha sauce

⅓ cup white sugar

Preparation:

1. Put all ingredients into a large-sized pitcher and whisk to dissolve the sugar.
2. Pour the mixture into the vessel of Ninja Slushi.
3. Select "FRAPPE". The preset will start at the default/optimal level.
4. If desired, adjust the temperature.
5. Once the frozen drink reaches the optimal temperature, the unit will beep.
6. Enjoy immediately with your favorite topping.

Vanilla Oat Frappé

Servings: 8

Ingredients:

1 cup plus 2 tablespoons extra creamy oat milk

1 cup plus 2 tablespoons oat creamer

4½ cups chilled black coffee

1 tablespoon vanilla extract

1 tablespoon ground cinnamon

¾ cup white sugar

Preparation:

1. Put all ingredients into a large-sized pitcher and whisk to dissolve the sugar.
2. Pour the mixture into the vessel of Ninja Slushi.
3. Select "FRAPPE". The preset will start at the default/optimal level.
4. Adjust the temperature control to illuminate 4 bars.
5. Once the frozen drink reaches the optimal temperature, the unit will beep.
6. Enjoy immediately with your favorite topping.

Caramel Coffee Frappé

Servings: 8

Ingredients:

2¼ cups half & half

4½ cups black coffee

¾ cup caramel sauce

⅓ cup white sugar

Preparation:

1. Put all ingredients into a large-sized pitcher and whisk to dissolve the sugar.
2. Pour the mixture into the vessel of Ninja Slushi.
3. Select "FRAPPE". The preset will start at the default/optimal level.
4. Adjust the temperature control to illuminate 4 bars.
5. Once the frozen drink reaches the optimal temperature, the unit will beep.
6. Enjoy immediately with your favorite topping.

Sweet Oat Caramel Frappé

Ingredients:

1 cup plus 2 tablespoons oat milk

1 cup plus 2 tablespoons vanilla oat creamer

4½ cups black coffee, chilled

¾ cup caramel sauce

⅓ cup white sugar

Preparation:

1. Put all ingredients into a large-sized pitcher and whisk to dissolve the caramel and sugar.
2. Pour the mixture into the vessel of Ninja Slushi.
3. Select "FRAPPE". The preset will start at the default/optimal level.
4. Adjust the temperature control to illuminate 3 bars.
5. Once the frozen drink reaches the optimal temperature, the unit will beep.
6. Enjoy immediately with your favorite topping.

Coffee Frappé

Ingredients:

5⅓ cups sweetened black coffee

1⅓ cups whole milk

1⅓ cups heavy cream

⅓ cup white sugar

2½ teaspoons vanilla extract

Preparation:

1. Put all ingredients into a large-sized pitcher and whisk to dissolve the sugar.
2. Pour the mixture into the vessel of Ninja Slushi.
3. Select "FRAPPE". The preset will start at the default/optimal level.
4. Adjust the temperature control to illuminate 4 bars.
5. Once the frozen drink reaches the optimal temperature, the unit will beep.
6. Enjoy immediately with your favorite topping.

Chocolate Frappé

Ingredients:

2½ cups half-and-half

5 cups black coffee

1 cup chocolate sauce

⅓ cup white sugar

Preparation:

1. Put all ingredients into a large-sized pitcher and whisk to dissolve the sugar.
2. Pour the mixture into the vessel of Ninja Slushi.
3. Select "FRAPPE". The preset will start at the default/optimal level.
4. Adjust the temperature control to illuminate 4 bars.
5. Once the frozen drink reaches the optimal temperature, the unit will beep.
6. Enjoy immediately with your favorite topping.

Matcha Latte Frappé

Servings: 8

Ingredients:

7⅔ cups store-bought matcha latte

⅓ cup heavy cream

⅓ cup white sugar

Preparation:

1. Put all ingredients into a large-sized pitcher and whisk to dissolve the sugar.
2. Pour the mixture into the vessel of Ninja Slushi.
3. Select "FRAPPE". The preset will start at the default/optimal level.
4. If desired, adjust the temperature.
5. Once the frozen drink reaches the optimal temperature, the unit will beep.
6. Enjoy immediately with your favorite topping.

Golden Milk Frappé

Ingredients:

7⅔ cups store-bought golden milk latte

⅓ cup heavy cream

⅓ cup white sugar

Preparation:

1. Put all ingredients into a large-sized pitcher and whisk to dissolve the sugar.
2. Pour the mixture into the vessel of Ninja Slushi.
3. Select "FRAPPE". The preset will start at the default/optimal level.
4. Adjust the temperature control to illuminate 4 bars.
5. Once the frozen drink reaches the optimal temperature, the unit will beep.
6. Enjoy immediately with your favorite topping.

Hazelnut Latte Frappé

Servings: 8

Ingredients:

7⅔ cups store-bought hazelnut latte

⅓ cup heavy cream

1 teaspoon vanilla extract

⅓ cup white sugar

Preparation:

1. Put all ingredients into a large-sized pitcher and whisk to dissolve the sugar.
2. Pour the mixture into the vessel of Ninja Slushi.
3. Select "FRAPPE". The preset will start at the default/optimal level.
4. Adjust the temperature control to illuminate 4 bars.
5. Once the frozen drink reaches the optimal temperature, the unit will beep.
6. Enjoy immediately with your favorite topping.

Vanilla Caramel Macchiato Frappé

Ingredients:

2¾ cups caramel macchiato creamer
3¼ cups black coffee

2 teaspoons vanilla extract
⅓ cup white sugar

Preparation:

1. Put all ingredients into a large-sized pitcher and whisk to dissolve the sugar.
2. Pour the mixture into the vessel of Ninja Slushi.
3. Select "FRAPPÉ". The preset will start at the default/optimal level.
4. Adjust the temperature control to illuminate 4 bars.
5. Once the frozen drink reaches the optimal temperature, the unit will beep.
6. Enjoy immediately with your favorite topping.

Peppermint Mocha Frappé

Servings: 8

Ingredients:

2¾ cups peppermint mocha creamer
3¼ cups black coffee

2 teaspoons vanilla extract
⅓ cup white sugar

Preparation:

1. Put all ingredients into a large-sized pitcher and whisk to dissolve the sugar.
2. Pour the mixture into the vessel of Ninja Slushi.
3. Select "FRAPPÉ". The preset will start at the default/optimal level.
4. Adjust the temperature control to illuminate 4 bars.
5. Once the frozen drink reaches the optimal temperature, the unit will beep.
6. Enjoy immediately with your favorite topping.

French Vanilla Frappé

Ingredients:

2¾ cups French vanilla creamer

3¼ cups black coffee

2 teaspoons vanilla extract

⅓ cup white sugar

Preparation:

1. Put all ingredients into a large-sized pitcher and whisk to dissolve the sugar.
2. Pour the mixture into the vessel of Ninja Slushi.
3. Select "FRAPPÉ". The preset will start at the default/optimal level.
4. Adjust the temperature control to illuminate 4 bars.
5. Once the frozen drink reaches the optimal temperature, the unit will beep.
6. Enjoy immediately with your favorite topping.

Cinnamon Coconut Frappé

Servings: 8

Ingredients:

1 cup plus 2 tablespoons full-fat coconut milk

1 cup plus 2 tablespoons coconut creamer

4½ cups chilled black coffee

1 tablespoon vanilla extract

1 tablespoon ground cinnamon

¾ cup white sugar

Preparation:

1. Put all ingredients into a large-sized pitcher and whisk to dissolve the sugar.
2. Pour the mixture into the vessel of Ninja Slushi.
3. Select "FRAPPÉ". The preset will start at the default/optimal level.
4. Adjust the temperature control to illuminate 4 bars.
5. Once the frozen drink reaches the optimal temperature, the unit will beep.
6. Enjoy immediately with your favorite topping.

Pumpkin Pie Latte Frappé

Ingredients:

7⅔ cups store-bought pumpkin pie latte

⅓ cup heavy cream

1 teaspoon vanilla extract

⅓ cup white sugar

Preparation:

1. Put all ingredients into a large-sized pitcher and whisk to dissolve the sugar.
2. Pour the mixture into the vessel of Ninja Slushi.
3. Select "FRAPPÉ". The preset will start at the default/optimal level.
4. Adjust the temperature control to illuminate 4 bars.
5. Once the frozen drink reaches the optimal temperature, the unit will beep.
6. Enjoy immediately with your favorite topping.

Vanilla Hazelnut Frappé

Servings: 8

Ingredients:

2¾ cups hazelnut creamer

3¼ cups black coffee

2 teaspoons vanilla extract

⅓ cup white sugar

Preparation:

1. Put all ingredients into a large-sized pitcher and whisk to dissolve the sugar.
2. Pour the mixture into the vessel of Ninja Slushi.
3. Select "FRAPPÉ". The preset will start at the default/optimal level.
4. Adjust the temperature control to illuminate 4 bars.
5. Once the frozen drink reaches the optimal temperature, the unit will beep.
6. Enjoy immediately with your favorite topping.

Chocolate Caramel Frappé

Ingredients:

2¾ cups chocolate caramel creamer

3¼ cups black coffee

2 teaspoons vanilla extract

⅓ cup white sugar

Preparation:

1. Put all ingredients into a large-sized pitcher and whisk to dissolve the sugar.
2. Pour the mixture into the vessel of Ninja Slushi.
3. Select "FRAPPÉ". The preset will start at the default/optimal level.
4. Adjust the temperature control to illuminate 4 bars.
5. Once the frozen drink reaches the optimal temperature, the unit will beep.
6. Enjoy immediately with your favorite topping.

Vanilla Cinnamon Frappé

Servings: 8

Ingredients:

2¾ cups cinnamon vanilla creamer

3¼ cups black coffee

2 teaspoons vanilla extract

⅓ cup white sugar

Preparation:

1. Put all ingredients into a large-sized pitcher and whisk to dissolve the sugar.
2. Pour the mixture into the vessel of Ninja Slushi.
3. Select "FRAPPÉ". The preset will start at the default/optimal level.
4. Adjust the temperature control to illuminate 4 bars.
5. Once the frozen drink reaches the optimal temperature, the unit will beep.
6. Enjoy immediately with your favorite topping.

Strawberry Latte Frappé

Ingredients:

7⅔ cups store-bought strawberry latte

⅓ cup heavy cream

1 teaspoon vanilla extract

⅓ cup white sugar

Preparation:

1. Put all ingredients into a large-sized pitcher and whisk to dissolve the sugar.
2. Pour the mixture into the vessel of Ninja Slushi.
3. Select "FRAPPÉ". The preset will start at the default/optimal level.
4. Adjust the temperature control to illuminate 4 bars.
5. Once the frozen drink reaches the optimal temperature, the unit will beep.
6. Enjoy immediately with your favorite topping.

Violet Latte Frappé

Servings: 8

Ingredients:

7⅔ cups store-bought violet latte

⅓ cup heavy cream

1 teaspoon vanilla extract

⅓ cup white sugar

Preparation:

1. Put all ingredients into a large-sized pitcher and whisk to dissolve the sugar.
2. Pour the mixture into the vessel of Ninja Slushi.
3. Select "FRAPPÉ". The preset will start at the default/optimal level.
4. Adjust the temperature control to illuminate 4 bars.
5. Once the frozen drink reaches the optimal temperature, the unit will beep.
6. Enjoy immediately with your favorite topping.

Chapter 8 Milkshake Recipes

Mocha Milkshake ………………………………… 91

Double Chocolate Milkshake ……………………… 91

Caramel Milkshake ……………………………… 92

Coffee Milkshake ………………………………… 92

Orange Creamsicle Milkshake …………………… 93

Hot Cocoa Milkshake …………………………… 93

Strawberry Milkshake …………………………… 94

Peppermint Milkshake …………………………… 94

Cherry Milkshake ………………………………… 95

Mango Milkshake ………………………………… 95

Vanilla Cream Milkshake ………………………… 96

Vanilla Coconut Milkshake ……………………… 96

Vanilla Chocolate Milkshake……………………… 97

Mango and Pineapple Milkshake ………………… 97

Mixed Berry Milkshake…………………………… 98

Chocolate Coffee Milkshake ……………………… 98

Delicious Pumpkin Spice Milkshake……………… 99

Vanilla Blueberry Milkshake …………………… 99

Amaretto Milkshake ……………………………… 100

Creamy Apple Milkshake ………………………… 100

Mocha Milkshake

Servings: 8

Ingredients:

4⅓ cups whole milk
2⅓ cups heavy cream
1 tablespoon vanilla extract

⅓ cup white sugar
⅔ cup mocha syrup

Preparation:

1. Put all ingredients into a large-sized pitcher and whisk to dissolve the sugar.
2. Pour the mixture into the vessel of Ninja Slushi.
3. Select "MILKSHAKE". The preset will start at the default/optimal temperature for ideal texture.
4. If desired, adjust the temperature.
5. Once the frozen drink reaches the optimal temperature, the unit will beep.
6. Enjoy immediately.

Double Chocolate Milkshake

Servings: 8

Ingredients:

4⅓ cups whole milk
2⅓ cups heavy cream
1 tablespoon vanilla extract

⅓ cup white sugar
⅔ cup chocolate syrup
½ cup cocoa powder

Preparation:

1. Put all ingredients into a large-sized pitcher and whisk to dissolve the sugar.
2. Pour the mixture into the vessel of Ninja Slushi.
3. Select "MILKSHAKE". The preset will start at the default/optimal temperature for ideal texture.
4. If desired, adjust the temperature.
5. Once the frozen drink reaches the optimal temperature, the unit will beep.
6. Enjoy immediately.

Caramel Milkshake

Ingredients:

4⅓ cups whole milk

2⅓ cups heavy cream

1 tablespoon vanilla extract

⅓ cup white sugar

⅔ cup caramel syrup

Preparation:

1. Put all ingredients into a large-sized pitcher and whisk to dissolve the sugar.
2. Pour the mixture into the vessel of Ninja Slushi.
3. Select "MILKSHAKE". The preset will start at the default/optimal temperature for ideal texture.
4. If desired, adjust the temperature.
5. Once the frozen drink reaches the optimal temperature, the unit will beep.
6. Enjoy immediately.

Coffee Milkshake

Servings: 8

Ingredients:

4⅓ cups whole milk

2⅓ cups heavy cream

1 tablespoon vanilla extract

⅓ cup white sugar

⅔ cup coffee syrup

Preparation:

1. Put all ingredients into a large-sized pitcher and whisk to dissolve the sugar.
2. Pour the mixture into the vessel of Ninja Slushi.
3. Select "MILKSHAKE". The preset will start at the default/optimal temperature for ideal texture.
4. If desired, adjust the temperature.
5. Once the frozen drink reaches the optimal temperature, the unit will beep.
6. Enjoy immediately.

Orange Creamsicle Milkshake

Ingredients:

2⅔ cup whole milk

1⅓ cups heavy cream

4 cups orange juice

2½ teaspoons vanilla extract

4 drops orange food coloring, optional

⅔ cup white sugar

Preparation:

1. Put all ingredients into a large-sized pitcher and whisk to dissolve the sugar.

2. Pour the mixture into the vessel of Ninja Slushi.

3. Select "MILKSHAKE". The preset will start at the default/optimal temperature for ideal texture.

4. If desired, adjust the temperature.

5. Once the frozen drink reaches the optimal temperature, the unit will beep.

6. Enjoy immediately.

Hot Cocoa Milkshake

Servings: 8

Ingredients:

1⅔ cups hot cocoa powder

6⅔ cups whole milk

1⅓ cups heavy cream

⅓ cup white sugar

Preparation:

1. Put all ingredients into a large-sized pitcher and whisk to dissolve the sugar.

2. Pour the mixture into the vessel of Ninja Slushi.

3. Select "MILKSHAKE". The preset will start at the default/optimal temperature for ideal texture.

4. If desired, adjust the temperature.

5. Once the frozen drink reaches the optimal temperature, the unit will beep.

6. Enjoy immediately.

Strawberry Milkshake

Servings: 8

Ingredients:

4⅓ cups whole milk

2⅓ cups heavy cream

1 tablespoon vanilla extract

⅓ cup white sugar

⅔ cup strawberry syrup

Preparation:

1. Put all ingredients into a large-sized pitcher and whisk to dissolve the sugar.
2. Pour the mixture into the vessel of Ninja Slushi.
3. Select "MILKSHAKE". The preset will start at the default/optimal temperature for ideal texture.
4. If desired, adjust the temperature.
5. Once the frozen drink reaches the optimal temperature, the unit will beep.
6. Enjoy immediately.

Peppermint Milkshake

Servings: 8

Ingredients:

6⅔ cups whole milk

1⅓ cups heavy cream

½ cup white sugar

3 tablespoons peppermint extract

Preparation:

1. Put all ingredients into a large-sized pitcher and whisk to dissolve the sugar.
2. Pour the mixture into the vessel of Ninja Slushi.
3. Select "MILKSHAKE". The preset will start at the default/optimal temperature for ideal texture.
4. If desired, adjust the temperature.
5. Once the frozen drink reaches the optimal temperature, the unit will beep.
6. Enjoy immediately.

Cherry Milkshake

Ingredients:

2⅔ cup whole milk

1⅓ cups heavy cream

4 cups cherry juice

2½ teaspoons vanilla extract

⅔ cup white sugar

Preparation:

1. Put all ingredients into a large-sized pitcher and whisk to dissolve the sugar.
2. Pour the mixture into the vessel of Ninja Slushi.
3. Select "MILKSHAKE". The preset will start at the default/optimal temperature for ideal texture.
4. If desired, adjust the temperature.
5. Once the frozen drink reaches the optimal temperature, the unit will beep.
6. Enjoy immediately.

Mango Milkshake

Ingredients:

4⅓ cups whole milk

2⅓ cups heavy cream

1 tablespoon vanilla extract

⅓ cup white sugar

⅔ cup mango syrup

Preparation:

1. Put all ingredients into a large-sized pitcher and whisk to dissolve the sugar.
2. Pour the mixture into the vessel of Ninja Slushi.
3. Select "MILKSHAKE". The preset will start at the default/optimal temperature for ideal texture.
4. If desired, adjust the temperature.
5. Once the frozen drink reaches the optimal temperature, the unit will beep.
6. Enjoy immediately.

Vanilla Cream Milkshake

Servings: 8

Ingredients:

5¾ cups whole milk

1 cup plus 2 tablespoons heavy cream

1 cup granulated sugar

2½ tablespoons vanilla extract

Preparation:

1. Put all ingredients into a large-sized pitcher and whisk to dissolve the sugar.
2. Pour the mixture into the vessel of Ninja Slushi.
3. Select "MILKSHAKE". The preset will start at the default/optimal temperature for ideal texture.
4. If desired, adjust the temperature.
5. Once the frozen drink reaches the optimal temperature, the unit will beep.
6. Enjoy immediately.

Vanilla Coconut Milkshake

Servings: 8

Ingredients:

6⅔ cups full-fat coconut milk

1⅓ cups full-fat coconut cream

1 cup white sugar

3 tablespoons vanilla extract

Preparation:

1. Put all ingredients into a large-sized pitcher and whisk to dissolve the sugar.
2. Pour the mixture into the vessel of Ninja Slushi.
3. Select "MILKSHAKE". The preset will start at the default/optimal temperature for ideal texture.
4. If desired, adjust the temperature.
5. Once the frozen drink reaches the optimal temperature, the unit will beep.
6. Enjoy immediately.

Vanilla Chocolate Milkshake

Ingredients:

4⅓ cups whole milk

2⅓ cups heavy cream

1 tablespoon vanilla extract

⅔ cup chocolate syrup

¼ cup white sugar

Preparation:

1. Put all ingredients into a large-sized pitcher and whisk to dissolve the sugar.
2. Pour the mixture into the vessel of Ninja Slushi.
3. Select "MILKSHAKE". The preset will start at the default/optimal temperature for ideal texture.
4. If desired, adjust the temperature.
5. Once the frozen drink reaches the optimal temperature, the unit will beep.
6. Enjoy immediately.

Mango and Pineapple Milkshake

Servings: 8

Ingredients:

2⅔ cup whole milk

1⅓ cups heavy cream

2 cups mango juice

2 cups pineapple juice

2½ teaspoons vanilla extract

⅓ cup white sugar

Preparation:

1. Put all ingredients into a large-sized pitcher and whisk to dissolve the sugar.
2. Pour the mixture into the vessel of Ninja Slushi.
3. Select "MILKSHAKE". The preset will start at the default/optimal temperature for ideal texture.
4. If desired, adjust the temperature.
5. Once the frozen drink reaches the optimal temperature, the unit will beep.
6. Enjoy immediately.

Mixed Berry Milkshake

Ingredients:

4 cups whole milk

2 cups heavy cream

2 teaspoons vanilla extract

¼ cup granulated sugar

½ cup mixed berries syrup

Preparation:

1. Put all ingredients into a large-sized pitcher and whisk to dissolve the sugar.
2. Pour the mixture into the vessel of Ninja Slushi.
3. Select "MILKSHAKE". The preset will start at the default/optimal temperature for ideal texture.
4. If desired, adjust the temperature.
5. Once the frozen drink reaches the optimal temperature, the unit will beep.
6. Enjoy immediately.

Chocolate Coffee Milkshake

Servings: 8

Ingredients:

4⅓ cups whole milk

2⅓ cups heavy cream

1 tablespoon vanilla extract

⅓ cup white sugar

⅔ cup coffee syrup

½ cup cocoa powder

Preparation:

1. Put all ingredients into a large-sized pitcher and whisk to dissolve the sugar.
2. Pour the mixture into the vessel of Ninja Slushi.
3. Select "MILKSHAKE". The preset will start at the default/optimal temperature for ideal texture.
4. If desired, adjust the temperature.
5. Once the frozen drink reaches the optimal temperature, the unit will beep.
6. Enjoy immediately.

Delicious Pumpkin Spice Milkshake

Servings: 8

Ingredients:

4 cups whole milk

2 cups heavy cream

2 teaspoons vanilla extract

¼ cup granulated sugar

½ cup pumpkin spice syrup

Preparation:

1. Put all ingredients into a large-sized pitcher and whisk to dissolve the sugar.
2. Pour the mixture into the vessel of Ninja Slushi.
3. Select "MILKSHAKE". The preset will start at the default/optimal temperature for ideal texture.
4. If desired, adjust the temperature.
5. Once the frozen drink reaches the optimal temperature, the unit will beep.
6. Enjoy immediately.

Vanilla Blueberry Milkshake

Servings: 8

Ingredients:

2⅔ cup whole milk

1⅓ cups heavy cream

4 cups blueberry juice

2½ teaspoons vanilla extract

⅔ cup white sugar

Preparation:

1. Put all ingredients into a large-sized pitcher and whisk to dissolve the sugar.
2. Pour the mixture into the vessel of Ninja Slushi.
3. Select "MILKSHAKE". The preset will start at the default/optimal temperature for ideal texture.
4. If desired, adjust the temperature.
5. Once the frozen drink reaches the optimal temperature, the unit will beep.
6. Enjoy immediately.

Amaretto Milkshake

Ingredients:

4⅓ cups whole milk

2⅓ cups heavy cream

1 tablespoon vanilla extract

⅓ cup white sugar

⅔ cup amaretto syrup

Preparation:

1. Put all ingredients into a large-sized pitcher and whisk to dissolve the sugar.
2. Pour the mixture into the vessel of Ninja Slushi.
3. Select "MILKSHAKE". The preset will start at the default/optimal temperature for ideal texture.
4. If desired, adjust the temperature.
5. Once the frozen drink reaches the optimal temperature, the unit will beep.
6. Enjoy immediately.

Creamy Apple Milkshake

Servings: 8

Ingredients:

2⅔ cup whole milk

1⅓ cups heavy cream

4 cups apple juice

2½ teaspoons vanilla extract

⅓ cup white sugar

Preparation:

1. Put all ingredients into a large-sized pitcher and whisk to dissolve the sugar.
2. Pour the mixture into the vessel of Ninja Slushi.
3. Select "MILKSHAKE". The preset will start at the default/optimal temperature for ideal texture.
4. If desired, adjust the temperature.
5. Once the frozen drink reaches the optimal temperature, the unit will beep.
6. Enjoy immediately.

In conclusion, the Ninja DoubleStack XL 2-Basket Air Fryer presents a seamless blend of practicality and innovation, revolutionizing cooking experiences across the board. Its intuitive design and consistent performance streamline meal preparation, while its contemporary aesthetic effortlessly integrates into any kitchen setting. Teamed with the Ninja DoubleStack XL 2-Basket Air Fryer Cookbook, users unlock a treasure trove of culinary inspiration, guiding them through a diverse array of recipes. Whether tackling weekday dinners or entertaining guests on weekends, this dynamic combination ensures delicious results with minimal hassle. From novice cooks to seasoned chefs, the Ninja DoubleStack XL 2-Basket Air Fryer and its companion cookbook empower individuals to explore and excel in the realm of air frying.

Appendix 1 Measurement Conversion Chart

VOLUME EQUIVALENTS (LIQUID)

US STANDARD	US STANDARD (OUNCES)	METRIC (APPROXIMATE)
2 tablespoons	1 fl.oz	30 mL
¼ cup	2 fl.oz	60 mL
½ cup	4 fl.oz	120 mL
1 cup	8 fl.oz	240 mL
1½ cup	12 fl.oz	355 mL
2 cups or 1 pint	16 fl.oz	475 mL
4 cups or 1 quart	32 fl.oz	1 L
1 gallon	128 fl.oz	4 L

VOLUME EQUIVALENTS (DRY)

US STANDARD	METRIC (APPROXIMATE)
⅛ teaspoon	0.5 mL
¼ teaspoon	1 mL
½ teaspoon	2 mL
¾ teaspoon	4 mL
1 teaspoon	5 mL
1 tablespoon	15 mL
¼ cup	59 mL
½ cup	118 mL
¾ cup	177 mL
1 cup	235 mL
2 cups	475 mL
3 cups	700 mL
4 cups	1 L

TEMPERATURES EQUIVALENTS

FAHRENHEIT(F)	CELSIUS(C) (APPROXIMATE)
225 °F	107 °C
250 °F	120 °C
275 °F	135 °C
300 °F	150 °C
325 °F	160 °C
350 °F	180 °C
375 °F	190 °C
400 °F	205 °C
425 °F	220 °C
450 °F	235 °C
475 °F	245 °C
500 °F	260 °C

WEIGHT EQUIVALENTS

US STANDARD	METRIC (APPROXINATE)
1 ounce	28 g
2 ounces	57 g
5 ounces	142 g
10 ounces	284 g
15 ounces	425 g
16 ounces (1 pound)	455 g
1.5 pounds	680 g
2 pounds	907 g

Appendix 2 Recipes Index

A

Amaretto Milkshake 100
Apple Beer Slushi 44
Apple Cider Frozen Juice Slushi 26
Apple Cider Whiskey Spiked Slushi 62
Apple Frozen Juice Slushi 77
Apple Iced Tea Slushi 52
Apricot Soda Slushi 41

B

Berry Frozen Juice Slushi 30
Blackberry Soda Slushi 43
Blue Raspberry Fruit Punch Slushi 14
Blueberry Iced Tea Slushi 54

C

Caramel Coffee Frappé 81
Caramel Milkshake 92
Chai Tea Slushi 48
Champagne Mango Spiked Slushi 65
Cherry Iced Tea Slushi 54
Cherry Lime Slushi 75
Cherry Milkshake 95
Cherry Slushi 75
Chocolate Caramel Frappé 88
Chocolate Caramel Spiked Slushi 67
Chocolate Coffee Milkshake 98
Chocolate Frappé 83
Chocolate Soda Slushi 44
Cinnamon Coconut Frappé 86
Citrus Fruit Punch Soda Slushi 38
Citrus Peach Slushi 21
Coconut Lemonade Spiked Slushi 78
Coconut Limeade Spiked Slushi 62
Coconut Pineapple Rum Spiked Slushi 66
Coffee Frappé 82
Coffee Milkshake 92
Cranberry and Apple Slushi 16
Cranberry Apple Slushi 76
Cranberry Concord Grape Frozen Juice Slushi 29
Cranberry Frozen Juice Slushi 32
Cranberry Iced Tea Slushi 56
Cranberry Limeade Slushi 21
Cranberry Mango Frozen Juice Slushi 26
Cranberry Pineapple Frozen Juice Slushi 33
Cranberry Rosé Wine Spiked Slushi 66

Cranberry Soda Slushi 45
Cranberry Strawberry Slushi 15
Cranberry Vodka Spiked Slushi 73
Cranberry Watermelon Frozen Juice Slushi 27
Cranberry-Grape Frozen Juice Slushi 72
Cranberry-Orange Frozen Juice Slushi 28
Cream Mocha Spiked Slushi 61
Creamy Apple Milkshake 100

D

Delicious Pumpkin Spice Milkshake 99
Double Chocolate Milkshake 91

E

Easy Cherry Frozen Juice Slushi 28
Easy Margarita Spiked Slushi 72
Easy Pineapple Orange Frozen Juice Slushi 34

F

French Vanilla Frappé 86
Fresh Peach Iced Tea Slushi 53
Fruit Punch Slushi 19
Fruity Rum Spiked Slushi 60

G

Ginger Ale Soda Slushi 37
Golden Milk Frappé 84
Grape Soda Slushi 39
Grapefruit Frozen Juice Slushi 25
Grapefruit Soda Slushi 43
Green Tea Slushi 47

H

Hard Kombucha Spiked Slushi 64
Hazelnut Latte Frappé 84
Homemade Orange Spritz Spiked Slushi 60
Homemade Pineapple Coconut Slushi 23
Homemade Pomegranate Limeade Slushi 18
Hot Cocoa Milkshake 93

L

Lemon Cola Soda Slushi 40
Lemon Iced Tea Slushi 53
Lemon Lime Soda Slushi 36
Lemon Matcha Tea Slushi 55
Lemon Probiotic Soda Slushi 40
Lemon Seltzer Slushi 19
Lemon Strawberry Seltzer Slushi 69
Lemonade Iced Tea Slushi 49
Lemony Cherry Seltzer Slushi 23

Lime Cherry Cola Soda Slushi 41
Lime Cola Soda Slushi 42
Lime Daiquiri Spiked Slushi 77
Lime Green Tea Slushi 55
Lime Seltzer Slushi 70
Limeade Iced Tea Slushi 49
Limeade Slushi 69

M

Mango and Pineapple Milkshake 97
Mango Coconut Lemonade Slushi 22
Mango Daiquiri Spiked Slushi 63
Mango Frozen Juice Slushi 31
Mango Iced Tea Slushi 51
Mango Lemonade Slushi 16
Mango Milkshake 95
Mango Pineapple Tropical Slushi 15
Matcha Latte Frappé 83
Matcha Tea Slushi 48
Mixed Berry Milkshake 98
Mixed Fruit Sports Drink Slushi 70
Mocha Frappé 80
Mocha Milkshake 91

O

Orange Creamsicle Milkshake 93
Orange Frozen Juice Slushi 31
Orange Lemonade Slushi 20
Orange Mango Rum Spiked Slushi 67
Orange Pineapple Frozen Juice Slushi 30
Orange Prosecco Spiked Slushi 78
Orange Red Wine Spiked Slushi 58
Orange Soda Slushi 38

P

Peach Champagne Spiked Slushi 59
Peach Iced Tea Slushi 51
Peppermint Milkshake 94
Peppermint Mocha Frappé 85
Pineapple Coconut Slushi 18
Pineapple Frozen Juice Slushi 29
Pineapple-Orange Rum Spiked Slushi 61
Pink Lemonade Slushi 71
Pomegranate Iced Tea Slushi 50
Pomegranate Orange Frozen Juice Slushi 33
Pumpkin Pie Latte Frappé 87
Pumpkin Spice Frappé 80

R

Raspberry Frozen Juice Slushi 34
Raspberry Iced Tea Slushi 52

Raspberry Lemonade Slushi 74
Red Cream Soda Slushi 45
Refreshing Lemonade Slushi 14
Root Beer Soda Slushi 39
Rosé Wine Spiked Slushi 58

S

Simple Cream Soda Slushi 37
Simple Strawberry Slushi 22
Strawberry Daiquiri Spiked Slushi 73
Strawberry Iced Tea Slushi 50
Strawberry Latte Frappé 89
Strawberry Lemonade Slushi 74
Strawberry Margarita Spiked Slushi 63
Strawberry Milkshake 94
Strawberry Rosé Wine Spiked Slushi 64
Sweet Mango Frozen Juice Slushi 27
Sweet Oat Caramel Frappé 82
Sweet Peach Slushi 17
Sweet Pomegranate Soda Slushi 42
Sweet Tea Slushi 47
Sweet-Sour Blue Lemonade Slushi 20

T

Tasty Espresso Martini Spiked Slushi 59
Tasty Orange Frozen Juice Slushi 76
Tropical Fruit Iced Tea Slushi 56
Tropical Pineapple Mango Frozen Juice Slushi 32

V

Vanilla Blueberry Milkshake 99
Vanilla Caramel Macchiato Frappé 85
Vanilla Chocolate Milkshake 97
Vanilla Cinnamon Frappé 88
Vanilla Coconut Milkshake 96
Vanilla Cotton Candy Soda Slushi 36
Vanilla Cream Milkshake 96
Vanilla Hazelnut Frappé 87
Vanilla Milkshake 71
Vanilla Oat Frappé 81
Violet Latte Frappé 89

W

Watermelon Frozen Juice Slushi 25
White Cranberry Slushi 17
White Wine Spiked Slushi 65

Made in United States
Orlando, FL
18 December 2024

55976303R00067